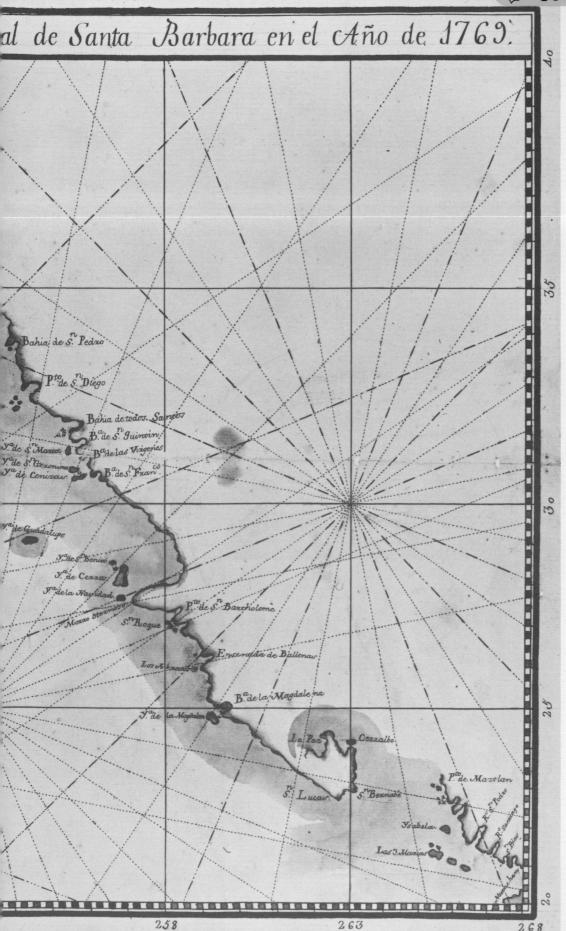

The map appearing as endpapers (inside cover) was the first map made to show the observations carried out by the Portolá expedition and reported by engineer Miguel Costansó in his letter to Don José de Gálvez—the man responsible for the expedition which "Founded California." It is a map of the California coast "corrected up to the Santa Barbara Channel" and drawn by Jorge Storace sailing master on the San Carlos in 1769.

The Henry E. Huntington Library graciously
gave permission to reproduce the map, letter,
inventory and portrait used in this book.

The Los Angeles Public Library graciously
gave permission to reproduce the
Costansó Narrative.

Series Consultant:
John D. Bruckman, Bibliographer
Los Angeles Public Library

Book One of the Hogarth Series of Early California

Standard Book Number 911776-04-4
Library of Congress Card Number 79-112869

THE COSTANSÓ NARRATIVE

OF THE PORTOLÁ EXPEDITION

First Chronicle of the Spanish Conquest
of Alta California

Translated, with an introduction
and bibliography,

by

Ray Brandes, Ph.D.

A Facsimile reproduction of the
original copy in the
Los Angeles Public Library

TABLE OF CONTENTS

LAST PAGE OF
GÁLVEZ CONFERENCE REPORT

The facsimile above is the last page of the report of the conference convoked by the Visitor-General of New Spain, Don José de Gálvez, at which it was decided to send expeditions from Lower California by land and sea to Upper California on a mission of occupation and colonization to found settlements in San Diego and Monterey.

It was these expeditions of 1769, with Don Gaspar de Portolá, Governor of Lower California in civil and military command and Father Junípero Serra as President of the Missions that were responsible for the establishment of the San Diego Mission, July 16, 1769 marking the "Founding of California."

Ray Brandes, Chairman, Department of History, University of San Diego obtained his Ph.D. from the University of Arizona at Tucson. His field of specialization is the American West, with other concentration of work in the Spanish Borderlands.

He has published works in these areas of history, and in archaeology; which include articles in *Arizona and the West, Southern California Historical Society Quarterly,* and *The Kiva.* He has served as editor of *Arizoniana:* the Journal of Arizona History, and of *Times Gone By,* the Journal of San Diego History.

Recent books published include the *Brand Book Number One,* San Diego Corral of the Westerners (editor); and two works scheduled for this year are *Fabric of Clay: The Biography of Frank Hamilton Cushing,* by the Arizona Historical Foundation, and an English version of Cayetano Alcazar's *Historia del Correo en America,* by the Western Postal History Museum.

Dr. Brandes is currently in charge of archaeological excavations at Mission San Diego de Alcalá, a project which began under his direction in 1966.

INTRODUCTION

The *Narrative* reproduced herein was written by Miguel Costansó, in the year 1770, while in the service of the Spanish Crown. The document is remarkable in that the author, an engineer and cosmographer, succinctly reported for the first time, within the pages of a single document, the founding of Alta California. Yet the Costansó *Narrative* is much more, for it relates concisely the events which led up to Spain's decision to occupy Alta California. The *Narrative,* with an engineer's precision, brings into focus the several arms of the expedition which otherwise become blurred as separate entities. The mind which made possible the *Narrative* belonged to a man of broad intellectual background, of intense perception, whose ability for detail was matched by an amazing capacity to view the broad spectrum of events and give those events meaning.

For several centuries before the *Narrative* was produced, Spanish officials had staked out claims to New World frontiers but without occupation. Spain stubbornly held to the unorthodox claims by "right of discovery." In 1542, Juan Rodriguez Cabrillo sailed in and out of San Diego Bay; and in 1602, Sebastian Vizcaino made outer-coast navigations. Other nations learned well the lessons of Spanish sea voyages, and within fifty years of the New World discovery had their vessels on the high seas.

The view of the British, French, Russians, and even the Dutch freebooters, however, held that mere discovery of land did not provide for ownership. Spanish officials well-knew of the Russian advance over the Urals, across Siberia, and into Alaska—a remarkable pattern of trapping and occupation by the *promysheleniki,* and the Cossacks—and a dangerous threat to Spanish claims on the Pacific coast. The Spanish Manila Galleon trade offered additional incentive to such as Spilberg's freebooters, to the commission of Sir Francis Drake and the *Golden Hind,* and to the explorations of the Russians on Alaskan coasts between 1741 and 1765.

During the Fifth Annual San Diego Historical Convention in March 1969, Professor Donald Cutter spoke of "Early Spanish Plans for the Occupation of Alta California," pointing out that the expeditions of 1769, had certainly not been the first to germinate in Spanish minds. From the time of Vizcaino, there had been plans to occupy Monterey on the Pacific. But continental wars, a generally-bankrupt Spanish treasury, an oft-lethargic Spanish government, and a resistance to budge on the theory of "right of discovery" brought delays.

"Defensive Spanish Expansion," as Professor Herbert Eugene Bolton has suggested, was the Spanish response when, in their view, a confrontation with Russia was near. Spaniards would move into the land to prevent encroachment. And thereby a web of events began to spin, which formed a dynamic historical situation: the founding of Alta California.

There remain innumerable enigmatic questions for Borderlands scholars to resolve. Certainly a most haunting figure is the author of the *Narrative,* Miguel Costansó. At the Historical Convention on "The Founding of Alta California," held at San Diego, in 1969, Professor Manuel Servin spoke of "Miguel Costansó: Forgotten Founder of California," and rightfully adjudged him as California's "first true historian." Professor Servin lamented the truth that a man who had given so much to the founding of California did not have a biography, and that not even his birth and death dates were a matter of record.

Miguel Costansó's life, as little as is known, has been gleaned from the few extant documents in his handwriting, and from the observations of his contemporaries. His cartography, the *Narrative,* and the 1769-1770 *diario* kept between San Diego and San Francisco Bay, however, provide much insight into his character.

He did not arrive in New Spain until the year 1764, but distinguished himself with the Corps of Engineers according to his superior officers. The next three to four years are a near blank in the record, but sometime probably late in 1767, José de Gálvez, Visitador-General to New Spain had Costansó complete a set of drawings of the Port of San Blas for submission to the Viceroy, and so the engineer and cosmographer could not have been an unknown quantity within the King's frontier service officers. His Plan of San Blas, finished in 1768, has been reproduced as a masterful piece of work. Costansó had a knowledge and grasp of the Mexican coastline and its possibilities as certainly no other person had during his time in Mexico.

In 1768 José de Gálvez, the single-most important figure in the development of the move to occupy Alta California, asked Costansó to be among an elite group of Spaniards who would meet at San Blas, to further develop those plans. At the meetings of the *Junta* in San Blas, Costansó did indeed find himself among a group of highly-trained and specialized men. In a document signed at San Blas on May 26, 1768, the *Junta* gave formal recognition to the Russian threat. The attestors to the document were José de Gálvez, Visitador-General; Miguel Costansó of the Royal

Corps of Engineers; Don Antonio Faveau de Quesada, Professor of Mathematics and Navigator of the Pacific waters and of the Philippines; Don Manuel Rivero Cordero, Naval Commandant; and Don Vicente Vila, Pilot first-class in the Royal Navy.[1]

During the meetings of the *Junta,* they in brief, set forth the details of the Gálvez masterplan of which the Visitador-General wrote to the Marqués de Croix.[2]

Miguel Costansó sailed with the Visitador-General to Baja California; and in 1768, while on the Peninsula made scale drawings of Bahias de La Paz, and Cerralvo.[3] Some of the details of the final days of preparation in Lower California can be found in the document "Noticias del Cavo de San Lucas. Ultimo termino de la California Meridional," written by Juan Manuel de Viniegra, José de Gálvez' secretary at Cabo San Lucas, on February 16, 1769.[4]

Costansó boarded the *San Carlos* captained by Vicente Vila, a native of Andalucia, and a sailing-master first-class in the Royal Spanish Navy. The vessel sailed from La Paz on January 10, 1769, and arrived at San Diego on April 29, 1769. As far as is known Costansó kept no diary or journal during that trip. In view of the letters he wrote on arrival at San Diego, however, he must have kept notes or records of some sort. His very training would have dictated such to him. Captain Vila did keep a diary which has been translated and published, which details that first leg of the expedition.

In a letter which he wrote to José de Gálvez, from the Port of San Diego on June 28, 1769, Miguel Costansó gave some most interesting details of the Spanish plight. He wrote of the feeble attempts being made to alleviate the suffering of those who were sick; gave interesting information about the landscape, water sources, and told of the natives in the vicinity.

When José de Gálvez earlier set forth the plans for the expeditions, he gave written and detailed instructions to each principal involved. At the Enseñada de Santa Barbara in the District of Santa Cruz on May 10, 1769, he gave such a document to Captain Don Domingo Antonio Callegari of the ill-fated *San José.* Within this he noted certain navigational aids:

> for the 34 degrees over the noted Port of San Diego which the observations of General Sebastian Vizcaíno and his pilots fixed at 33 degrees of latitude, and the Derrotero of Pilot Cabrera Bueno gave as 34 degrees . . . (and) ultimately this Packetboat is destined (the Port of Monterey, as the two boats which left earlier had this instruction—the third volume of the *Noticia de Californias* where there is included the account of the voyage of General Vizcaino, taken from Padre Torquemada, of that account left written by Fray Antonio de la Concepción Religioso Carmelita who was on that expedition of Vizcaino as one of the Chaplains of his vessels and second cosmographer for observations and charts. . . . [5]

11

At San Diego, on June 28, 1769, Miguel Costansó wrote to José de Gálvez an eleven page report in which he said:

> . . . I have not omitted to gather the necessary data in order to prepare as time permits, the plans, maps, and records which Your Illustrious Señor has charged me to undertake, for the correction of the older Derroteros with which I am experimenting differ somewhat and seem to be in error: In the first place the Port of San Diego is not found, nor ought to be looked for, at 33 degrees as Vizcaino says much less at 34 degrees in which the Pilot Cabrera Bueno situated it. . . . [6]

Obviously Costansó had been at work, and the document elaborates on the harbor with minutè attention to detail. Within two weeks he had been chosen to accompany the Governor, Gaspar de Portolá to search for the Port of Monterey, and on July 14, 1769, that party left overland. Costansó was ill—either with scurvy as then thought, or with dietary deficiency diseases as is now believed—but his close friend, the Surgeon Pedro Prat, advised him to make the journey, as a remedy.

Within that two week period at San Diego, Costansó made a trip up Mission Valley, and as noted in his *Narrative,* visited a number of Indian rancherías. He did prepare a map or plan of that valley showing among other features the location of such villages. The map, at some time, has been detached from the rest of the document. If located it would provide a wealth of information, badly sought after, both by anthropologists and historians.

From the moment he left San Diego with Portolá to search for Monterey he maintained a diary. Despite the hardships encountered, he faithfully and with the most careful of his skills kept that diary until the party returned to San Diego on January 24, 1770.[7] With all forces at hand, the Governor despatched a troop to Lower California for supplies and livestock; the *Aan Antonio* went to Mexico and later returned with provisions; all hands felt secure in the notion that forces should again be sent toward Monterey.

On April 16, 1770, Costansó, Father Serra and others embarked for Monterey, arriving there on May 31. A land expedition had arrived there on May 23, 1770.[8] The Governor managed to keep his chief engineer busy drawing plans for the Mission and Presidio, for Costansó's time at this newly-founded Port would be short. The Governor turned over the government to Pedro Fages; Portolá, Juan Pérez, Miguel Piño, and Miguel Costansó sailed for Mexico on the *San Antonio* on July 9, 1770. They stopped at San Blas on August 1, 1770; Pérez and Costansó then made their way to Mexico City allegedly arriving there about the 10th of August.[9]

During the next few years Costansó became involved in a number of enterprises. He distinguished himself in survey work; gave advice on solving problems related to supply ships for Alta California, helped to select new supply ports, and in 1775, recommended that Acapulco be chosen as Spain's west coast naval headquarters. On this score, he pointed out to his superiors the deficiencies of San Blas, but was ignored.

When asked by the Viceroy, Costansó gave advice on matters of defense and population of Upper California; he designed some of the outstanding government buildings in Mexico City, and drew up the plans to remodel the Alcázar or palace, of Chapultepec for the proposed archives; since he had been appointed Municipal Engineer, Costansó planned the drainage of Mexico City and held responsibility for the paving and repairing of the streets of that ancient capital.

In the 1770's, he became involved in consultations and sought-after advice by the Viceroy, when Juan Bautista de Anza sought permission to make the overland expeditions from Tubac Presidio to Alta California. Through the work of Costansó and others, Anza did make those expeditions, in 1774-1776, with settlers. And in 1776, gave his opinion relative to the expedition of Dominguez Escalante.[10]

Costansó continued as an engineer in the viceregal government in the capitol of New Spain; in the years 1793 and 1795, he made recommendations for the fortification of the California presidios.[11] Then, as mysteriously as he had arrived, Miguel Costansó disappeared. The last known reference is his report on the "Division of the Provinces of California into two, la Nuevà y la Antigua, California," written at Vera Cruz in 1802.[12]

The *Narrative* of Costansó presents one of those unique opportunities for examination. The author was not unlike most chroniclers of New Spain who took notice of the climate, geography, ecology, and the native inhabitants. The Spaniard by habit was addicted to writing: to penning personal letters in vehement prose, to keeping diaries and journals with attention to detail, to preparing reports and accounts so as to insure no suspicion be cast upon them—all in accord with the traditions of Royal Spanish regulations. Since each record was submitted to higher ecclesiastical or secular authority either in California, Mexico, or Spain, copies of the documents had to be made, often by other individuals. So it is today that copies of a single document are often found in different foreign and domestic archives.

The handwriting of the 17th and 18th New World Spaniard is extremely pleasing to the eye. In addition—though not entirely exceptional for the times—the writing is unerringly informative, and demonstrates a high degree of competence in the arts of language. Nonetheless, documents are often difficult to read because of the idioms, because of the changes in spelling of words which have come about through the passing of time, and because of the characteristic flourish of the script. Since the documents were often hurriedly written, and were time consuming in preparation, many abbreviations were insinuated into the documents, although the Costansó *Narrative* contains remarkably few such instances. The prob-

13

lems of the translator then, are compound but quite as absorbing as they are real.

The *Narrative,* as taken from the printed edition of Mexico City, reflects but the experiences of man: the bitterness and discouragement when food was low or when all did not go well, the high peaks of gratification for abundance or for something well-done. In the translating and editing of the *Narrative,* I have attempted to preserve a faithful reflection of the thoughts and descriptions of Miguel Costansó. I have made certain changes in the text in keeping with modern grammar and capitalization. The writer himself was not always consistent in the use of accents or punctuation. Sentences written and then put in print in the Mexico City edition are always extremely long, are involved and compounded sentences which tend to confuse the reader. These have been shortened, maintained as separate thoughts whenever possible. Within the printing there are typographical errors, preserved within the document but not within the translation. The editing then, has been in the tradition of making the document readable and interesting, but without changing the essential literary character or thought of the writer.

The *Narrative* is a contradiction to the *Diarios* kept by Costansó and others during the 1769 expeditions. On his initial voyage to San Diego on the *San Carlos,* Costansó kept no diary or journal; such apparently was left to Captain Vicente Vila. When Costansó went to search for Monterey with Governor Portolá, he began at once to keep a *diary* which records that phase of the expeditions—which he maintained until the return to San Diego on January 24, 1770. This *diary,* signed at the Port and Presidio of San Diego on February 7, 1770 has been published in several editions. To this he gave the title: *Diary of the Journey by land made to the north of California by Order of His Excellency the Marqués de Croix, Viceroy, Gov. and Capt. General of New Spain, Etc., Etc.; by instruction of the Most Illustrious Don Joseph de Gálvez, of the Council and Court of His Majesty in the Supreme Council of the Indies, Inspector-General of all the Tribunals, Royal Exchequers, and Departments of Finance of His Majesty in the Same Kingdom, and Intendant of the Kings Army Etc., Etc.; performed by the troops detailed for this purpose under the command of the Governor of the Peninsula of California, Don Gaspar de Portolá, Captain in the Dragoons of the Spanish Regiment.*

The best translation of the *diario* is that edited by Frederick J. Teggart, as *The Portolá Expedition of* 1769-1770: *The Diary of Miguel Costansó,* Academy of Pacific Coast History, vol. 2, no. 4, in Publications, Berkeley, 1911

The *Narrative* is signed in Mexico City, by Costansó, on October 24, 1770. From San Diego on June 28, 1769, he wrote de Gálvez that he was making notes and gathering data. According to Theodore E. Treutlein, in his *San Francisco Bay: Discovery and Colonization, 1769-1776,* California Historical Society, 1968, Costansó wrote to de Gálvez on February 7, 1770, and mentioned his *diary* stating:

(it) lacks the introduction and end, which I formed separately. . . . It also lacks being tied and bound up with that of the sea (the diary of the sea voyage to San Diego) which I still have only in rough draft.[13]

Costansó left Monterey and arrived in the capitol about August 10, 1770. Sometime then, between February 7, 1770, the identical date on which he signed his *Diario and* wrote to Gálvez, and October 24, 1770, Costansó worked on the *Narrative.* That it is a combination of his notes kept at sea, the letters which he wrote to Gálvez, and a boiled-down version of a *Diario* seems clear. Between February and October 1770, he had indeed, added an introduction, and an ending, and he had tied up his land diary with a sea account.

To the *Narrative* Costansó gave a slightly different title: *The Historical Diary of the voyages by sea and land made to the north of California by Order of His Excellency Marqués de Croix, Viceroy, Governor, and Captain-General of New Spain and by Direction of His Most Illustrious Señor Don Joseph de Gálvez of the Council and Court of His Majesty, in the Supreme Council of the Indies, Quartermaster General, Visitador-General of this Kingdom, carried out by the troops destined for said purpose under the command of Don Gaspar de Portolá, Captain of Dragoons in the Regiment of Spain, and Governor in said Peninsula, and by the packetboats the San Carlos and the San Antonio, under the command of Don Vicente Vila, Pilot of the first-class in the Royal Navy, and of Don Juan Pérez, of the Navigation of the Philippines.*

When was the *Narrative* first printed? Hubert Howe Bancroft, *History of California* (vol. XVIII in the *Works)* states that Costansó published this account in Mexico, in 1770. The edition by Adolph Van Hemert-Engert and Frederick J. Teggart, *The Narrative of the Portola Expedition* . . . , indicates the British Museum Catalogue accepts the date of 1770. In that same volume, p. 93, the editors indicates that while the manuscript is dated October 24, 1770, it is not known when the book was actually published. "Robert Green . . . says it was published at Mexico in 1771, and immediately suppressed by the government." The work translated by Herbert I. Priestley, *A Historical . . . Description of California by Pedro Fages,* states on pp. vii-viii that:

> . . . dated October 24, 1770; it is to be inferred that it was printed immediately thereafter. Certainly it appeared earlier than November 20, 1775, for on that date Fages, concluding the *continuación y suplemento, said that the Diario Histórico had* already been printed.

Zamorano Eighty: A Sketch of Distinguished California Books, Made by the Members of the Zamorano Club of Los Angeles, 1945, discusses the publication of the Costansó *Narrative,* in this case referring to it as the *Diario,* with the information that Costansó:

> made a map embodying the results of this expedition which is now in the Museo Naval, Madrid. It was engraved in the following year by Hipólito Ricarte and published by Tomás López. This map was dated: Mexico, October 30, 1770, and accompanied a letter by the viceroy addressed to Julian de Arriaga dated October 28. With this letter the viceroy enclosed a copy of the printed *Diario.* It is therefore plain that it had been printed between October 24 and October 28, 1770. (Arriaga was the Minister of the Indies and Marina.)

Ellen Barrett's *Bibliography* (I), indicated "En el Imprenta del Superior Gobierno, 1776. . . . Cowan's *Bibliography.* . . . (I), indicated that the precise date is not known and that it is believed the work was suppressed by the Spanish government immediately on its appearance as it contained certain information of use to navigators of other nationalities. This author has seen several printed copies of the *Narrative,* but none give a date of publication; only the date of October 24, 1770, when Costansó signed the document. One could speculate that on the basis of Known *Casa de Contratación* (House of Trade) methods of operation, which in Spain, held the reins over commerce, navigation and cartography, that authorities would most likely have insisted on the suppression of a printing, if in fact one had been accomplished in 1770. Suppressed on the basis that the *Narrative* would have provided Spain's enemies with too much data. Would she have gloated over the expeditions—hardly—the weakened condition of the small forces of Spain on the Pacific, the navigational data, and other vaulable information would have been too revealing.

In any case the consensus seems to be that the *Narrative was* published shortly after the Costansó signature was applied on October 24, 1770; surely the reason is as enigmatic as the author himself.

Almost all bibliographers agree that an edition titled: *An Historical Journal of the Expeditions by sea and land, to the North of California, in 1768, 1769, and 1770; when Spanish establishments were first made at San Diego and Monte-Rey, from a Spanish Ms,* was translated by William Reveley, Esq., published by A. Daylrmple, and printed in London in 1790. Several authorities note that "Espedicion á Californias, años 1768, 1770," appeared in *El Album Mexicano,* Vol. II, pp. 37-40, 1849, signed at the end, "M.P." This is referred to as the brief notes on the "Costanzó Expedition."

A translation of this *Narrative* was accomplished by Charles Fletcher Lummis under his "Early California History" section in *The Land of Sunshine* June and July 1901, and titled "The Expedition of 1769."

Perhaps the most available edition to date, however, is that one edited by Adolph Van Hemert-Engert and Frederick J. Teggart, as vol. 1, no. 4, in *Publications* of the Academy of Pacific Coast History, Berkeley, University of California, 1910, titled: *The Narrative of the Portolá Expedition of 1769-1770 by Miguel Costansó."* Another edition was published in Mexico, 1950, under the title of *Miguel Costansó's Diario histórico de los viages de mar y tierra hechos al norte de la California, escrito por Miguel Costansó en el año de 1770.* This was published by Edición Chimalistac.

Douglas S. Watson, in cooperation with the remarkable Grabhorn Press published a splendid work in 1934, titled: *The Spanish Occupation of California: Plan for the Establishment of a Government. Junta or Council held at San Blas, May 16, 1768. Diario of the Expeditions made to California, Plan and Junta have been translated from the Spanish documents by D. S. Watson and T. W. Temple II, and the Diario of M. Costansó follows the translation of F. J. Teggart.* The latter portion of this volume includes the Costansó *Narrative.*

"The most recent appearance of the Diario Histórico appears on pp. 77-123 (with a facsimile of the title page of Colección Chimalistic, vol. 5, *Noticias y documentos acerca de las Californias, 1764-1795,* edited by W. Michael Mathes, published in Madrid in 1959 by Ediciones José Porrúa Turanzas.

One can hope and speculate that the scholars working in the field of the Spanish Borderlands will locate diaries kept by expedition members yet missing, and to see to their publication; that yet unknown diaries or reminiscences may be found; and that some will take up the banner for the writing of more biographies of California's founders. The Archivo de Indias in Seville, the Archivo Histórico Nacional in Madrid, The Archivo General of Mexico City, and the Bancroft Library at Berkeley hold many clues. Aside from those biographies related to Father Junípero Serra, almost no other personality of the founding year has received a study which has been published. Gaspar de Portolá, Fernando Javier Rivera y Moncada, Juan Pérez, Vicente Vila, and Miguel Costansó merit just such attention. These men may become a bit better known through the bibliography of 1769-1770 *Diarios,* and the selected bibliography which follows.

NOTES

**One military document giving the military service record of Miguel Costansó is located in the AGI, "Mexico Seccion," No. 2472.

[1]HM José de Gálvez, GA 419, Huntington Library.

[2]HM José de Gálvez, GA 463 and 509, Huntington Library. See also Herbert I. Priestley, *José de Gálvez . . . ,* who cites 14 documents from Gálvez to Croix, San Blas, May 18 to 24, in Archivo de Indias, 104-6-14. *(estante* 104, *cajón* 6, *legajo* 14).

[3]Chapman, *Catalog . . . ,* Item 1041, letter July 30, 1768, Marqués de Croix to Arriaga, no. 319; Item 1066, Sept. 1, 1768, at Real de Santa Anna. Miguel Costansó, "Relación del reconocimiento de la Bahia de San Bernardo en el Cavo de San Lucas . . . con expresion de las providencias, que parecen mas oportunas, y conducentes al resguardo de este puerto." 104-3-2; and Item 1768, circa Sept. 1, 1768, Costansó and Joseph de Urrutia, Plano de la Bahia de sn Bernabé en el Cabo de San Lucas. 104-3-2.

[4]Copy in Bejar archives of the Univ. of Texas, William B. Stephens Collection, no. 145; see also Chapman, *Catalog . . . ,* Items 1168, 1169, 1170, Jan. 5, 1769, from Gálvez to Vila, Fages, and Costan-

só, 104-3-2: Item 1413, Dec. 18, 1769, from San Blas—Juan Pérez and Joseph Paredes (no. 2), "Memoria de los efectos y vivires que se embarcar en el paquebot de S.M. nombrado *sn Antonio* alias *el Princîpe,* con destino a la Mision y escolta de sn Carlos de Monterrei, 104-3-3; Dec. 18, 1769, Item 1414, San Blas, Juan Pérez y Joseph Paredes, "Memoria de los efectos, vivires, y utiles se embarcan en el paquebot de S.M. *el Princîpe* con destino á la expedicion de tierra de Monterrey á entregar en aquel puerto al Theniente de Voluntarios de Cataluña dn Pedro Fages, 104-3-3.

[5]José de Gálvez to Captain Domingo Callegari from Enseñada de Santa Barbara May 10, 1769, HM José de Gálvez, 592, Huntington Library.

[6]Costansó to Gálvez, San Diego June 28, 1769, HM José de Gálvez, 583, Huntington Library; see also Bolton, *Guide . . . ,* vol. 66, "California Section" in Archivo General de la Nación, Viceroy to Costanso, March 11, 1769.

[7]See Chapman, *Catalogue . . . ,* Item 1337, July 14 to Feb. 7, 1770, San Diego, Miguel Costansó, Diario de la expedicion hecha por tierra desde el puerto de San Diego al norte de California en descubierto del de Monterrey, Año de 1769 y 1770, May 2, 1770, Mexico, 200 pp. 104-3-3; Item 1338, July 14 to January 24, 1770, dated Feb. 7, 1770, at San Diego, Miguel Costansó, Diario historico de los viages de mar y tierra hechos al norte de la California . . . por la tropa distinada al mando de Gaspar de Portolá . . . y los paquebots S. Carlos y S. Antonio al mando de Vicente Vila . . . y D. Juan Pérez, 214 pp., Estado and Guadalajara 1, Doc. 7. Item 1449, San Diego, Feb. 7, 1770, Pedro Fages & Costansó to the Marqués de Croix (No. 2) gives an account of events in Upper California since the arrival of expeditions at San Diego, 3 pp. 104-3-3; Item 1450, San Diego Feb. 11, 1770, Gaspar de Portolá to the Marqués de Croix (no. 1), a relation of the northward journey from San Diego and return, 8 pp. 104-3-3; and Bolton, *Guide . . . ,* letter from Costansó to Gálvez, Feb. 8, 1770, in vol. 66, "California Section," Archivo General; and "Costansó's diary of the Portolá expedition to California, 1769-1770," in vol. 396, "Historia Section," Archivo General.

[8]Bolton, *Guide . . . ,* Letter Costansó and Fages to the Viceroy, April 14, 1770; in vol. 66, "California Section," Archivo General; letter Costansó and Fages to the Viceroy from Monterey, June 13, 1770, in *do;* Chapman, *Catalog . . . ,* letter Junípero Serra to Gálvez from Monterey, July 2, 1770, on possession of Monterey, 104-3-3.

[9]Bolton, *Guide . . . ,* letter Costansó to Viceroy, from San Blas, Aug. 2, 1770, in vol. 66, "California Section," Archivo General.

[10]Bolton, *Guide . . . ,* Communication of Costansó concerning California, Mexico City, Sept. 5, 1772, vol. 36, "California Section," Archivo General. Bolton, on page 7, of his Historical Sketch, notes that "Costansó executed the plans for remodeling the Alcázar, or palace, of Chapultepec, chosen as a safe place from fire, dampness and disturbances, (as a proposed archives). Bolton also lists Miguel Costansó comments of Oct. 9, 1772, as Noticias de la misiones de los nuevos establecimientos, in Vol. 13, "California Section," Archivo General; and "Opinion of Costansó relative to expedition of Dominguez Escalante," written at Mexico City, March 18, 1776, in vol. 52, "Historia Section," Archivo General: and "Opinions of Costansó concerning disturbances from New Mexico to Monterey and Sonora," at Mexico City, March 18, 1776, in vol. 169, "Provincias Internas Section," Archivo General.

[11]Ltr, October 17, 1794, Pinart Ms, 193-219, Bancroft Library. Also, Bolton, *Guide . . . ,* "Opinion made in *junta particular* for defense of the Californias, July 11, 1795 by Costansó and Salvador Fidalgo in vol. 47, "California Section," Archivo General.

[12]Bolton, *Guide . . . ,* "Division of Provinces of California into two, la Nueva y la Antigua, California," by Miguel Costansó, of Vera Cruz, 1802, in vol. 180, "Provincias Internas Section," Archivo General.

[13]Treutlein, p. 17, note 19, cites Costansó to Gálvez, in Bolton papers, Alta California, Item No. 90, folder 19, Bancroft Library.

A portrait of Don José de Gálvez, who in 1769 zealously fitted out the expeditions which succeeded in making the first settlements in Upper California thus "Founding California."

DIARIO HISTORICO

DE LOS VIAGES DE MAR, Y TIERRA

HECHOS AL NORTE DE LA CALIFORNIA

DE ORDEN

DEL EXCELENTISSIMO SEÑOR

MARQUES DE CROIX,

Virrey, Governador, y Capitan General de la
Nueva Eſpaña:

Y POR DIRECCION

DEL ILLUSTRISSIMO SEÑOR

D. JOSEPH DE GALVEZ,

Del Conſejo, y Camara de S. M. en el Supremo de
Indias, Intendente de Exercito, Viſitador General
de eſte Reyno.

Executados por la Tropa deſtinada à dicho objeto al mando

DE DON GASPAR DE PORTOLÀ,

Capitan de Dragones en el Regimiento de Eſpaña, y Governador
en dicha Peninſula

Y por los Paquebots el S. Carlos, y el S. Antonio al mando

DE DON VICENTE VILA,

Piloto del Numero de primeros de la Real Armada,

Y DE DON JUAN PEREZ,

de la Navegacion de Philipinas.

DE ORDEN DEL EXCmo. SR. VIRREY,
En la Imprenta del Superior Gobierno.

NOTICIOSO EL ALTO GObierno de España de las repetidas Tentativas de una Nacion Extrangera sobre las Costas Septentrionales de la California, con miras nada favorables á la Monarquia, y á sus Intereses, mandó el REY al Marqués de Croix, su Virrey, y Capitan General en la Nueva España diese eficazes Providencias para resguardar *aquella* parte de sus Dominios de toda Invasion, é Insulto.

Havia facilitado el Marqués de Croix las Ideas del Monarca sobre este asunto; pues antes de recibir esta Orden, y al tiempo de la Expulsion de los Jesuitas de Nueva España, tenia nombrado Governador Politico, y Militar de la California, para que executara la misma Operacion en aquella Provincia, la mantuviera bajo la Obediencia del Soberano, la conservara en paz, y diera aviso de qualquiera novedad, que ocurriese.

Igualmente havia resuelto S. Excia. embiar á dicha Peninsula Sugetos Inteligentes, que dedicados unicamente á reconocer, y recorrer lo descubierto de ella, le informasen del estado de sus Misiones, de la disposicion,

A   ca-

calidad, y numero de fus Naturales, de fu modo de vivir, y conftumbres de las producciones proprias de aquella Tierra, de la naturaleza de fus Minas, del metodo que fe feguia en fu Laborío, de quienes las disfrutaban, que Poblaciones de Efpañoles, ó Gente de otras Caftas havia eftablecidas, y finalmente de la calidad, y naturaleza de fus Coftas, Puertos, y Mares para dar en virtud de eftos informes, y previas noticias las ordenes, y providencias conducentes al fomento, y arreglo del Comercio, Minería, y Poblacion de aquellos Paifes.

Pero al pafo, que S. Excia. conocia la necefsidad de eftos Informes, para proceder con acierto en la execucion de fus defignios, fe hallaba tambien indecifo en la dificultad de nombrar Sugetos, en quienes concurrieffen las circunftancias que requeria femejante Comifion para fu defempeño: quando á impulfos del proprio zelo, que animaba á S. Excia. levantó el pefo de efta dificultad el Illmo. Sr. D. Jofeph de Galvez, deftinado á vifitar las Provincias de Cinaloa, y Sonora, ofreciendo ir Perfonalmente á Californias con el defeo de llenar tan altas Ideas, y poner en execucion unos Proyectos, cuyo argumento confideraba de la mayor importancia.

Aplau-

Aplaudió, y admitió S. Excia. la genero-
fa oferta del Illmo. Sr. Galvez, y dandole todas fus vezes, tanto en lo Militar, como en lo
Politico, á fin de que por sí, fegun la necefidad,
y ocurrencias, aplicafe á dichos afuntos oportunas providencias, y reglamentos, difpufo el
Sr. Vifitador General fu Viage, y falió de Mexico el nueve de Abril de mil fetecientos fefenta y ocho.

Por Mayo de el proprio año llegó fu S.
Illma. al Puerto de San Blas, Aftillero, y Poblacion erigidos nuevamente fobre la Cofta
de la Nueva Galicia en la Mar de el Sur, en
donde fe havian fabricado las Embarcaciones
deftinadas á la Navegacion, y Comercio de
la Sonora; y en la actualidad fe eftaban conf-
truyendo otros Buques, que debian, fegun las
intenciones de efte Govierno, fervir á la comunicacion, y trato de la California.

Bajando á efte Puerto con el fin de embarcarfe para aquella Peninfula alcanzaron á
fu S. Illma. unos pliegos de Mexico, en que el
Sr. Virrey incluía la orden, que recientemen-
te havia recibido de la Corte, concerniente el
cuydado, y vigilancia con que importaba mi-
rar, y celar las Coftas Occidentales de la California, y S. Excia. añadió la oportuna providencia, de que el Sr. Vifitador defpachafe una

B   Ex-

Expedicion Marítima al famoſo Puerto de Monterrey.

Era el reſguardo, y cuſtodia de las Coſtas de la California, uno de los objetos que ocuparon dignamente la atencion del Excmo. Sr. Marques de Croix, y con eſte motivo recomendaba nuevamente á ſu S. Illma. un punto, cuya importancia ſe hechaba de ver en la eſtimacion, que le añadia la orden del Monarca, dejando al prudente arbitrio del Sr. Viſitador el aplicar los medios que juzgaſe mas oportunos, y conducentes á tan recomendable fin.

Pero antes de referir los que puſo por obra el Illmo. Sr. D. Joſeph de Galvez, ſe hace preciſo decir algo de las Coſtas de la California, objeto de las atenciones del Govierno, manifeſtando aſsi miſmo el eſtado de la Peninſula, y en general el de los negocios de la Mar del Sur al arribo de ſu S. Illma. à San Blas, para dar á conocer el acierto de las providencias, ſu proporcion con ellos, y con los pocos recurſos, ſobre que ſe puede contar en tan remotas Tierras.

Son conocidas por el nombre de Exteriores, ú Occidentales de la California, aquellas Coſtas de la America Septentrional, que regiſtran el Occeano Aſiatico, ó ſea Mar del Sur, y diſcurren ſobre ſus Aguas el largo eſpacio

de-

demas de quinientas leguas Maritimas entre
el Cabo de San Lucas, por veinte, y dos grados y quarenta, y ocho minutos de Latitud, y
el Rio de los Reyes, por quarenta y tres grados; citamos al Rio de los Reyes, no como li-
mite, pero sí como termino de lo descubierto de ellas, por los Navegantes de nuestra
Nacion; aunque no se estienda à tanto lo Con-
quistado, y reducido por los Españoles à la
obediencia de su Augusto Monarca, cuyo Do-
minio, no reconocen aun todas las Naciones
comprehendidas dentro de la Peninsula, si su
garganta, ó parte por donde queda unida al
Continente, se considera entre la boca del
Rio Colorado, y el Puerto de San Diego, dos
puntos, que con leve diferiencia, coinciden
bajo del Paralelo de treinta, y dos grados,
y medio.

Lo reducido de la California, empezan-
do desde el Cabo de San Lucas, llegaba sola-
mente hasta los treinta grados, y medio de Latitud, en que se halla la Mision de Santa Maria, à corta distancia de la Bahia de San Luis
Gonzaga, Puerto muy acomodado, y seguro
sobre el Mar de Cortés, ò Seno Californio;
pero todo este tramo estaba à penas Poblado
de otra Gente, que de sus mismos Naturales,
congregados muy pocos de ellos en las Mi-

sio-

6

siones, y difperfos los demàs en diferentes Rancherias vagantes que reconocian, como à Cabezera la Mifion mas inmediata; eftos cuyo numero es bien limitado, à excepcion de hallarfe Catequizados, y hechos Chriftianos, confervaban en lo reftante el mifmo modo de bufcar la vida, que en fu Gentilidad, en la caza, ò en la pefca, viviendo por los Montes, para recoger las Semillas, y Frutas, que ofrece la Tierra, fin cultivo alguno.

La Gente Efpañola, y otras Caftas, llamadas de razon en la America, y eftablecidas dentro de la Peninfula, no llegaba à quatrocientas Almas, incluiendo en efte numero à las Familias de los Soldados del Prefidio del Loreto, y las de algunos, que fe decian Mineros, que havitaban à la parte del Sur, de donde fe infiere quan poco podia contarfe fobre fus Moradores para la defenfa de fus Coftas, y la facilidad que ofrecia à qualefquiera Eftrangeros para eftablecerfe fobre ellas, fin recelo de hallar opoficion alguna, mayormente fi huviefen intentado el defembarco azia el Norte en los celebrados Puertos de San Diego, y Monterrey, cafo que traía configo fatales refultas; pudiendo tomar pofefion de la Tierra, y fortificarfe en dichos Parages, fin que llegafe, ò llegafe tarde, à noticia del

del Govierno, y hallandofe el daño en terminos de irremediable.

Sobre la Mar del Sur en todo lo que mira à las Coſtas de la Nueva Eſpaña, no ſe conocian otras Embarcaciones, que los Paquebots, recien conſtruidos en San Blas, y otros dos de pequeño porte, que ſirvieron à los Miſioneros expulſos de la California, para ſu comunicacion, con las vecinas, y fronteras Coſtas de la Sonora, y Nueva Galicia. En eſtos pocos Buques conſiſtian todas las fuerzas Maritimas, que ſe pudieſen oponer à las invasiones Extrangeras.

A viſta pues de la orden con que ſe hallaba ſu Señoria Illmà. y de los eſcaſos medios, que ofrecia aquella Provincia coñociendo igualmente, que no era dable practicar por el pronto lo mejor, no por eſto deſiſtiò de el empeño en que ſe hallaba, antes venció con induſtria la dificultad, dividiendo los inconvenientes; ſintiò la neceſidad de Poblar lo deſcubierto de la California de Gente util, capaz de cultivar ſus tierras, y aprovecharſe de las ricas produciones que ofrece en Minerales, grana, ó otros frutos, como aſimiſmo de tomar las Armas en defenſa de ſus Caſas, ſiempre que llegaſe el caſo, pero ſiendo tan dilatados, como ſe dixo, los Paiſes comprehendidos,

C   vajo

vajo el nombre de California, no era menos
necefario adelantar todo lo pofible para el
Norte nuevos eftablecimientos, que dandofe
la mano con los del Sur, pudiefen mutuamente foftenerfe.

    Nadie ignora las repetidas, y coftofas
expediciones, que para realizar efte proyec-
to, y reconocer la Cofta Occidental de la California, fe hicieron en los dos Siglos antece-
dentes; el acierto, y felicidad, que tuvo la ultima executada en el año de mil feifcientos, y
dos, por el General Sebaftian Vizcayno, lo-
grando defcubrir los Puertos de San Diego, y
Monterrey, fituados aquel, por treinta, y dos
grados, y medio de Latitud, y efte por treinta
y feis, y quarenta minutos, de cuya refulta di-
manó la Real Cedula del Sr. Phelipe Tercero
en que mandaba ocupar, y poblar el Puerto
de Monterrey; cuya utilidad fe conoció bien
defde entonces, cometiendo efta importante Comifion al mifmo Sebaftian Vifcayno;
pero aunque las Ordenes de aquel Monarca
eftaban dadas con tal acuerdo, y concebidas
en terminos, que parecian allanar toda dificultad, y vencer todo impofible, no fe llevaron à debido efecto, fin que pueda decirfe, que
impedimentos ocafionaron fu inobfervancia,
aunque muriefe Vifcayno quando fe difponia
à la Emprefa.
                      Los

Los miſmos motivos Politicos que en aquel tiempo ſe tuvieron preſentes para expedir ahora dichas Ordenes, y agregandoſe los otros que van referidos, dictaba la prudencia el partido que convenia ſeguir en las actuales circunſtancias, para lograr el mejor acierto.

Con eſta mira, reſolvió el Illmó. Señor Don Joſeph de Galvez en Junta, que preſidió en San Blas el diez, y ſeis de Mayo de mil ſetecientos ſeſenta, y ocho, con aſiſtencia del Comandante de aquel Departamento, de los Oficiales de Exercito, y Pilotos, que ſe hallaban en él, que ſe volbieſe á dicha Empreſa con mayores fundamentos, ocupando de una vez los Puertos de S. Diego, y Monterrey, eſtableciendo en ellos Preſidio, y Miſion, y aſegurando con eſta providencia la Poſeſion de aquella Tierra á nueſtro Auguſto Soberano, contra las pretenciones de hueſpedes Eſtrangeros; y reſervó ſu Illmà. para tiempo mas oportuno aumentar aquellos eſtablecimientos, y darles toda la ſolidèz que conviene.

Quedó pues reſuelta la expedicion Maritima, y deſtinados los Buques, en que havia de executarſe, eligiendo à eſte efecto el San Carlos, y el San Antonio, como Vaſos de mayor porte, y reſiſtencia; pero como ſu Señoria Illmà. huvieſe de paſar à la California, para

deſde

defde allí tomar nuevas medidas, y dar varias
ordenes al mifmo intento, difirió por entonces nombrar à los Oficiales, y Tropa, que havian de llevar de tranfporte juntamente con
los Padres Mifioneros que fe havian de facar
de dicha Peninfula.

Hallabanfe à la fazon fuera de San Blas
los dos Paquebots, y fe confideraban navegando la vuelta del Puerto, del que falieron en
Marzo del proprio año, con tranfporte de Tropa para el de Guaymas en la Provincia de Sonora; por lo que dejando al Comandante de
aquel Departamento las ordenes conducentes
al breve defpacho, y habilitacion de las citadas
Embarcaciones, fe embarcó fu S. Illmà. para la
California el dia veinte, y quatro de Mayo en
la Balandra la Cinaloa, y en cinco de Julio,
tomó Tierra en la Bahia Cerralbo, defpues de
haver reconocido por sí mifmo las Iflas Ifa-
bela, y Marias, y el Puerto de Mazatlan en
la Cofta de Cinaloa.

Mientras tanto fe acopiaba todo lo necefario para tan dilatado, y penofo Viage; pero aunque el Comandante de San Blàs, y los
demás Sujetos encargados de efte importante
afunto anduvieron muy folícitos, contra toda dilacion, la tardanza de los Barcos en ref-
tituirfe al Puerto, por razon de los vientos

con-

contrarios, y la dificultad, que por la mifma caufa experimentaron defpues en fu Viage, para pafar à la California, atrafó notablemente la Expedicion Maritima.

Entre tanto trabajaba, con incanfable defvelo el Señor Vifitador General, y fobrando en la California afuntos de grave importancia, dignos de ocupar fu atencion, nunca perdió de vifta la proyectada Empresa, cuyo buen exito quifo afegurar por quantos caminos podian tentarfe, y por quantos medios le fugeria fu difcurfo: no le pareció fuficiente à fu S. Illmà. la Expedicion Maritima, para obtener, y llegar al fin que fe proponia; confideraba los infinitos riefgos, y contratiempos á que iban expueftas las Embarcaciones en una navegacion dilatada, y que podia decirfe nueva por las efcafas noticias, que de ella fe tenian; las enfermedades, que podian afaltar á las Tripulaciones frequentes en Viages largos, y otras contingencias inevitables, de cuyas reflexiones nació la refolucion de embiar por Tierra otra Expedicion, que dirigiendofe à los mifmos deftinos, que la Maritima, pudiefe preftar, ó recibir de efta, fegun las ocurrencias, los focorros, de que mutuamente necefitafen.

A efte fin defpachò fu S. Illmà. à todas las Mifiones de la Peninfula, con encargo à los

D   Re-

Reverendos Padres Miniftros de ellas, para que por fu parte contribuyefe cada uno con los efectos, de que fin hacerle falta pudiefe defprenderfe en Ornamentos, y Vafos Sagrados para las nuevas Mifiones, Frutas fecas, y Caldos para dichos Viages, Caballeria, y Mulada.

Las Provifiones, y Viveres para el Viage de Tierra fe embarcaron en el Prefidio del Loreto abordo de quatro Lanchones Tripulados de intento, para llevarlos à la Bahía de San Luis Gonzaga, de donde pafaron à la Mifion de Santa Maria, ultima, y la mas avanfada al Norte, nombrada como punto de reunion, y partida azia donde iba tambien encaminandofe la Tropa, Harrieros, y Baqueros con el Ganado de toda efpecie, que fe havia de llevar en pie para carga, y para Poblar los Eftablecimientos proyectados.

Componiafe efta Tropa de quarenta Hombres de la Compañia de Californias, á que fe juntaron otros treinta Indios voluntarios de las Mifiones, armados de arco, y flechas: todas havian de marchar á las Ordenes del Governador de la Peninfula Don Gafpar de Portolà; pero halló fu S. Illma. por mas conveniente componer de ella dos Trozos. El Capitan de el Prefidio del Loreto D. Fernando Rivera,

vera, y Moncada, havia de conducir el primero en calidad de Explorador con veinte y cinco Hombres de fu Tropa, y algunos Indios Amigos, llevando el Ganado Bacuno; y el Governador Comandante en Gefe de la Expedicion havia de feguir defpues con el refto de la Gente, y Provifiones.

La falida del primer Trozo, conforme á las difpoficiones dadas por fu S. Illma. havia de efectuarfe á principios de Diciembre, pero la afpereza de los Caminos, la dificultad de juntar el Ganado, y de conducirlo por Tierras efcafas de paftos, y aguajes, como fon las del Norte de la antigua California, retardó confiderablemente la marcha, y el Ganado Bacuno, que llegó á la Mifion de Santa Maria á principios de Marzo de fefenta y nueve, quedó totalmente impofibilitado de profeguir el Viage, de fuerte, que fue forzofo dexarlo en Velicatá, para que fe reforzara, difiriendo á mejor ocafion el conducirlo, como fe executó defpues.

Fundófe en Velicatá nueva Doctrina con la Advocacion de San Fernando por fer efte Parage, que difta como veinte leguas de la Mifion de Santa Maria, muy frequentado de las Naciones Gentiles del Norte de la California: dejófe en él la Efcolta fuficiente, y def-

de aqui ſiguiò ſu marcha para San Diego el primer Trozo de la Expedicion de Tierra el dia
veinte, y quatro de Marzo de dicho año.

El ſegundo Trozo de dicha Expedicion,
que conducia el Gobernador, ſalió de eſte miſmo parage de Velicatá en quince de Mayo,
llevando en ſu compañia al Preſidente de las
Miſiones de la California el Reverendiſimo
P. Fr. Junipero Serrà, que en una edad aban-
zada, ni los trabajos exceſivos, é inſeparables
de tan dilatado Viage, ni los que le eſpera-
ban en ſu apetecido Apoſtolado de Monterrey, fueron capazes de contener el ardiente
zelo, de que vive poſeido para la converſion
de aquella infinita Gentilidad al conocimiento
del verdadero Dios, y de ſu Santa Ley de
Gracia.

Los Paquebots el San Carlos, y el Principe, que ſegun las Ordenes de ſu S. Illmà. havian de tocar en el Puerto de la Paz en la California Meridional, para deſde él ſalir con la
Tropa Veterana de deſembarco, utiles, Per-
trechos, y Viveres para los nuevos Eſtablecimientos de San Diego, y Monterrey, tardaron en llegar à aquel Puerto, por la cauſa
que ſe inſinuó al principio. Entró el San Carlos à mediado de Diciembre, y como huvieſe trabajado mucho en la Mar forcejando con

los

los vientos, se le afloxaron, y escupió de las costuras alguna Estopa por donde venía haciendo agua. No era este accidente para dejado à las espaldas, y se juzgó indispensable el darlo à la vanda, para descubrirle el Costado, y la Quilla; operacion que tenia su dificultad en un Pais poco menos que destituido de quanto se necesitaba para el efecto: Executòse sin embargo acalorandola su S. Illmà. con su presencia, y exemplo, y en menos de quince dias recibió el Buque toda su carga, y quedando en disposicion de hacerse à la Vela, se embarcò la Tropa, que consistia en veinte, y cinco Hombres de la Compañia franca de Voluntarios de Cataluña con su Teniente D. Pedro Fages, que su S. Illmà. habia mandado venir del Exercito, ò Expedicion de Sonora. el Ingeniero D. Miguel Constansò, y el Cirujano D. Pedro Prat: embarcòse tambien para la asistencia espiritual de todos el muy Reverendo Padre Fr. Fernando Parron, Religioso del Colegio de *Propaganda Fide* de San Fernando de Mexico, que havia de quedarse en San Diego para fundar aquella Mision.

A este tiempo se tuvo noticia del otro Paquebot el San Antonio, que hallandose ya muy cerca del Puerto, fué Sotaventado por un viento recio del Norueste, y se viò obligado à arribar al Pulmo parage, y furgidero, que tiene algun refguardo de dicho viento en la Cofta del Sur de la Peninfula, defde donde fu Capitan Don Juan Perez, dió avifo de efte acaecimiento. Receló entonces fu S. Illma. que durando en fu fuerza los Norueftes, no deca- yefe mas à Sotavento, fi intentafen fus Pilo- tos ganar el Puerto, en cuya atencion defpa- chó Orden à dicho Capitan, para que pafara à la Bahía de San Bernabé, fituada en el Cabo de San Lucas, fobre la mifma Cofta, y la parte mas Meridional de la Peninfula, á donde fu S. Illma. refolvió transferirfe en el Paquebot la Concepcion.

Hicieronfe à la Mar à un tiempo la Con- cepcion, y el San Carlos defde el Puerto de la Paz, en diez de Henero de mil fetecientos fe- fenta y nueve, navegaron en conferva hafta el catorze del mifmo, en cuyo dia entraron, y dieron fondo en la Bahía de San Bernabé; pero no haviendo llegado aun el San Antonio, re- folvió fu S. Illma. mandar por delante al San Carlos, y al dia figuiente por la tarde zarpó efte Paquebot fus anclas, y fe hizo á la Vela para San Diego.

El San Antonio llegó á la exprefada Ba- hía de San Bernabé en fines de Henero, y aun- que no trahía incomodidad alguna, refolvió el

Sr.

Sr. Viſitador darlo tambien á la vanda para recorrer ſus coſtados, y habilitado como el San Carlos ſe hizo á la Mar para el miſmo deſtino en quince de Febrero.

Tiene la navegacion de la Coſta Exterior de la California una dificultad inſeparable en la conſtancia de los vientos Nortes, y Norueſtes, que con poca interrupcion duran todo el año, y ſon directamente opueſtos al Viage, por hallarſe tendida dicha Coſta de Norueſte, Sueſte, lo que preciſa á toda Embarcacion á retirarſe de ella, y enmararſe haſta dar con vientos mas variables, y propicios, con los quales elevandoſe para el Norte lo que neceſitan, logran recalar á Barlovento de el Puerto, á que ſe dirigen.

Bajo de eſte preſupueſto, y con orden de ſeguir el metodo indicado, hicieron ſu Viage al Puerto de San Diego los dos Paquebots, ſi bien con diſtinta fortuna, porque el San Carlos experimentó tanta contrariedad de vientos, y calmas, que viendoſe enmarado á mas de doſcientas leguas de la Coſta, y falto de agua, huvo de arrimarſe á ella para buſcarla: hizola en la Isla de Cerros con grande dificultad, y trabajo, manteniendoſe el Barco á la Vela, bordeando entre la Tierra firme, y la Isla, que no tiene abrigo, ni ſurgidero alguno donde ſe

pue-

pueda echar una ancla, fin exponerfe á per-
derla, por la mala calidad del fondo.

Concluida fu aguada, fe hizo de nuevo
á la Mar en veinte, y feis de Marzo, y el dia
veinte, y nueve de Abril entró en el Puerto
de San Diego á los ciento, y diez dias de haver
falido del de la Paz: pero fu Tripulacion, y la
Tropa de Tranfporte, cuya fatiga, en tan dilatado, y penofo Viage, y en lo mas crudo del
Invierno, no pudo menos que fer excefiva, llegaron en deplorable eftado. El Efcorbuto, in-
ficionò à todos, fin excepcion, de fuerte, que al
entrar en San Diego havian muerto ya dos
hombres de dicha enfermedad, lo mas de la
Gente de Mar, y la mitad de la Tropa fe hallaban poftrados en fus Lechos; folo quatro
Marineros quedaban en pie, y acudian, ayu-
dados de la Tropa à marear, y aferrar las Velas, y demas maniobras.

El Paquebot San Antonio, con haver
falido un mes defpues que el San Carlos, tuvo
la fortuna de rendir el Viage en cinquenta, y
nueve dias, y fe hallaba en dicho Puerto de San
Diego defde once de Abril, pero tenia la mitad de fu Tripulacion igualmente afecta del
Efcorbuto, de cuyo accidente havian muerto
tambien dos Hombres. En medio de tanta enfermedad tuvieron todos á felicidad grande el
jun-

juntarſe, y de comun acuerdo, deſpues de ha-
verſe amarrado el San Carlos en parage conveniente, reſolvieron los Oficiales atender
al pronto alivio de los Enfermos.

Fue la primera diligencia buſcar un
aguage de donde ſurtirſe, y llenar la Barrile-
ria de buena agua para el uſo de la Gente; á
cuyo fin el dia primero de Mayo deſembarca-
ron los Oficiales D. Pedro Fages, D. Miguel
Coſtanſó, y el ſegundo Capitan del San Carlos D. Gorge Eſtorace con la Tropa, y Marineros, que ſe hallaban con mas actitud para la
fatiga en numero de veinte, y cinco Hombres,
y ſiguiendo la Rivera Occidental del Puerto,
deſcubrieron á poco trecho una Tropa de Indios Armados de arco, y flechas, á quienes hicieron ſeña con paños blancos llamandolos
para tomar lengua; pero eſtos midiendo ſu paſo ſobre el de nueſtra Gente, no permitieron
en mas de media hora, que les dieran alcanze,
ni tampoco fue poſible à los nueſtros hacer
mayor diligencia, porque iban debiles, y deſpues de tan larga navegacion havian como
perdido el uſo de los pies. Parabanſe eſtos Indios de rato, à rato ſobre alguna altura obſer-
vando á la Gente, y dando à conocer el miedo
que les cauſaban los Foraſteros en lo miſmo,
que hacian para encubrirlo: hincaban la una

F   pun-

punta de ſus arcos en el ſuelo, y aziendolo por
el otro extremo baylaban, y daban vueltas al
rededor con indecible velozidad, pero luego
que veían á nueſtra Gente cerca volbian à ale-
jarſe con la miſma ligereza: ultimamente ſe
conſiguió atraerlos con deſpachar hazia ellos
à un Soldado, que deponiendo ſus Armas en
Tierra, y uſando de ademanes, y ſeñales de
Paz, conſintieron, que ſe arrimaſe: repartióles
eſte algunas dadibas mientras llegaban los demas, que acabaron de aſegurar aquellos Gentiles con algunos regalos mas quantioſos de
Cintas, Abalorios, y Buguerias. Pidieronles
por ſeñas donde eſtaba el aguage, y ellos ſe-
ñalando hazia à una Arboleda, que ſe diviſaba
à lo lejos para el Nordeſte, dieron á entender,
que entre ella corria algun Rio, ó Arroyo, y
que ſiguieſen, que los llevarian á èl.

Anduvieron coſa de tres leguas haſta
llegar à las orillas de un Rio ceñido por una,
y otra vanda de una Zeja de Sauzes, y Alamos
muy frondoſos, tendria ſu Caja veinte varas
de ancho, y deſaguaba en un Eſtero, que en
plea Mar podia recibir la Lancha, y daba comodidad para hacer la aguada: entre la Arboleda havia variedad de Arbuſtos, y Plantas
odoriferas como el Romerillo, la Salvia, Roſales de Caſtilla, y ſobre todo cantidad de Par-
ras

ras Silveftres, que á la fazon eftaban en flor.
El Pais era de afpecto alegre, y las Tierras de
las immediaciones del Rio parecieron de excelente migajon, y capaz de producir toda efpecie de frutos. El Rio bajaba de unas Sierras
muy altas por una Cañada efpaciofa, que fe
internaba la vuelta del Efte, y Nordefte: á tiro de fufil defviado de él, y fuera del Monte,
fe defcubria un Pueblo, ó Ranchería de los
mifmos Gentiles, que guiaban à los nueftros,
compuefto de varias enramadas, y Chozas de
figura Piramidal cubiertas de Tierra. Al avif-
tar á fus Compañeros con la Comitiva, que
trahían falieron todos â recibirlos Hombres,
Mugeres, y Niños, convidando con fus Cafas
á los Huefpedes: venian las Mugeres en trage
honefto cubiertas de la cintura hafta la rodilla
con redes tupidas, y dobles. Llegaronfe los Efpañoles al Pueblo, que conftaria de treinta á
quarenta Familias, y á un lado de él fe repara-
ba una Cerca hecha de ramas, y troncos de
Arboles, en donde dieron á entender que fe
refugiaban para defenderfe de fus Enemigos,
quando fe veían acometidos, fortificacion inexpugnable á las armas ufadas entre ellos.

Son eftos Naturales de buen talle, bien
difpueftos, y agiles, van defnudos fin mas ro-
pa, que un ceñidor texido en forma de red de

ixtle, ó pita muy fina, que facan de una planta llamada Lechuguilla: fus carcaxes que fugetan entre el ceñidor, y el cuerpo fon de pieles de Gato Montés, Coyote, Lobo. ó Gamo, y fus arcos tienen dos varas de largo; á mas de eftas armas ufan de una efpecie de macána de madera muy dura, cuya forma es femejante á la de un fable corto, y corbo, que arrojan de canto, y rompe el ayre con mucha violencia: defpidenla á mayor diftancia, que una piedra, fin él nunca falen al Campo, y fi ven à una Vibora, ú otro Animal nocivo le tiran la macána, y comummente lo parten de medio á medio. Segun experimentaron defpues en el trato continuo que con ellos tuvieron nueftros Efpañoles, fon de genio altivo, atrevidos. codiciofos, burlones, y baladrones, aunque de poco animo, hacen grande alarde de fus fuerzas, y tienen por mas esforzado al mas forzudo; fe perecen por qualefquiera trapo, pero con haver veftido á diferentes de ellos en repetidas ocafiones al dia figuiente fe prefentaban en cueros.

Hay en la Tierra Venados, Verrendos, muchas Liebres, Conejos, Ardillas, Gatos Montefes, y Ratas; abundan las Tortolas torcafas, las Codornices, Calandrias, Senfontles, Tordos, Cardenales, y Chupamirtos, Grajos, Cuer-

Cuervos, y Gavilanes, Alcatrazes, Gabiotas, Buzos, y otras Aves de rapiña Maritimas; no faltan Patos, ni Anzares de diferentes hechuras, y tamaños. Hay variedad de Pescados, los mejores son el Lenguado, y la Solla, que sobre ser de gusto delicado son de extraordinario tamaño, y pesan de quince á veinte libras; en los meses de Julio, y Agosto se coge tanto Bonito como se quiere. En todo el año hay Meros, Burgaos, Cavallas, Cazones, Rayas, Almejas, y Mariscos de todas especies: en los meses de Invierno acude la Sardina en tanta abundancia como en las Costas de Galicia, y Ayamonte. El principal sustento de los Indios que habitan la Rivera de este Puerto es de Pescado, comen mucho marisco por la mayor facilidad, que tienen en cogerlo; usan Balsas de Enea, que manejan diestramente con Canalete, ó remo de dos palas: sus fisgas son de unas varas largas, cuya punta es de hueso muy agusado, embutido en la madera, tan diestros en arrojarla, que rarisima vez yerran tiro.

    Reconocido el aguaje se restituyeron los Españoles abordo de las Embarcaciones, y como estas se hallasen muy retiradas del Estero en que desagua el Rio, resolvieron sus Capitanes D. Vicente Vila, y D. Juan Perez, arrimarse á él quanto pudiesen para dar me-

nos

nos que hacer á la Gente en el manejo de las Lanchas: hicieronſe eſtas faenas con harto trabajo, porque de un dia á otro, iba creciendo el numero de los Enfermos, al paſo que ſe morian los mas agravados, y aumentaba la fatiga de los pocos que quedaban en pie.

Conſtruyóſe en las immediaciones de la Playa á la parte del Eſte un corto recinto formado de un parapeto de tierra, y fagina, que ſe guarneció con dos Cañones: deſembarcaronſe algunas velas, y toldos de los Paquebots con las que ſe hicieron dos Tiendas capazes para Hoſpital: puſieron á un lado las ſuyas los dos Oficiales, los Padres Miſioneros, y el Cirujano, y hallandoſe todo en eſtado de recibir los Enfermos ſe trajeron de abordo en las Lanchas, y ſe acomodaron en las Tiendas lo mejor que ſe pudo.

Pero no fueron baſtantes eſtas diligencias á procurarles la ſalud, faltaban ya las Medicinas, y dietas que ſe conſumieron caſi todas durante la Navegacion: el Cirujano Don Pedro Prat ſuplia en el modo poſible ſu falta con algunas yervas, que buſcaba con mil afanes por los Campos, de cuya virtud tenia conocimiento, y de que neceſitaba èl miſmo, tanto como los Enfermos, hallandoſe poco menos que poſtrado de la miſma dolencia que ellos.

ellos. El frio se hacia sentir con rigor de noche en las Barracas, y el Sol de dia; alternativas que hacian sufrir cruelmente à los Enfermos: muriendose todos los dias dos, ò tres de ellos, y se vió reducida toda esta Expedicion, que se componia de mas de noventa Hombres à solo ocho Soldados, y otros tantos Marineros en estado de acudir al resguardo de los Buques, manejo de las Lanchas, Custodia del Real, y servicio de los Enfermos.

No havia noticia alguna de la Expedicion de Tierra, haviansse registrado las immediaciones del Puerto, buscando rastro de Caballada, pero no se descubrió ninguno, y no se sabia que pensar de su tardanza. Pero el dia catorce de Mayo los Indios dieron aviso á unos Soldados, que estaban en la Playa, que venian de la parte del Sur del Puerto unos Hombres Armados como ellos, y explicaban muy bien por señas, que venian montados en Caballos. Alegraronse todos con esta noticia, que se verificó de allí á poco avistandose la Gente, y la Requa del primer Trozo de la Expedicion de Tierra. Saludaronse mutuamente con festiva Salva de sus Armas, explicando despues con los brazos, y las voces su contento, que fue igual de una parte, y otra, porque todos esperaban hallar reciproco alivio en sus necesida-

des:

pes: venia toda la Gente de Tierra, sin haver perdido un Hombre, ni traer un Enfermo, despues de una marcha de dos Meses, pero à media Racion, y sin mas Provisiones que tres Costales de Harina de que se les subministraban por toda Racion diaria dos Tortillas á cada Individuo.

Descansaron aquel dia junto al Real de los Enfermos: surtieronse de bastimentos con que reparar sus fuerzas; y convinieron los Oficiales en transferir el Alojamiento cerca del Rio, lo que no se havia practicado antes, porque no pareciò acertado dividir las pocas fuerzas con que se hallaban, empleadas al resguardo mutuo de los Buques, y de la Gente alojada en Tierra, atendiendo asimismo, á la mayor comodidad, y brevedad de los Transportes para no fatigar excesivamente à los que manejaban la Lancha, y à que la falta de Bestias de carga, precisaba llevar á hombros quanto se echaba en la Playa.

Mudaronse todos al nuevo Real, que se transfirió una legua mas al Norte à la derecha del Rio sobre una Loma de mediana altura, donde se pudo atender con mas cuidado à los Enfermos, que el Cirujano D. Pedro Prat, no dejaba un instante, y asistia con suma caridad: pero viendo que no se lograba mejoria algu-

alguna en ellos, y que llegaria el cafo de que por falta de Marineros, los dos Paquebots fe impofibilitarian á falir del Puerto, fe penfó feriamente en defpachar à uno de ellos á San Blas con Pliegos para informar al Excmò. Sr. Virrey, y al Illmò. Sr. Vifitador General del eftado de ambas Expediciones.

Fue nombrado D. Juan Perez, Capitan del Principe para el efecto, refolviendo D. Vicente Vila quedarfe en San Diego hafta recibir nueva Orden, y el focorro de Gente que necefitaba, para executar lo que los Superiores determinafen.

Defcargòfe el Paquebot: tranfportaronfe al Real parte de los efectos: transbordaronfe los demas al San Carlos: aparejófe, y hallandofe ya en difpoficion de hacerfe á la Vela, llegó el Governador D. Gafpar de Portolá con el fegundo Trozo de la Expedicion de fu mando el dia veinte, y nueve de Junio.

Enteròfe luego del eftado de las cofas de San Diego, y defeofo que la Expedicion de Mar fe llevafe á debido efecto, propufo á D. Vicente Vila darle diez, y feis Hombres de la Gente de fu mando para feguir fu Viage á Monterrey: pero como entre ellos no havia ninguno que fuefe Marinero, no pudo Vila admitir fu oferta, mayormente havien-

H   do

do perdido á todos sus Oficiales de Mar, Contramaeſtre, Guardian, y Patron de Lancha, ſin tener de quien hechar mano para reemplazarlos.

Y conſiderando el Governador, que el accidente inopinado de los Barcos no le diſpenſaba de ſeguir ſu Viage à Monterrey por Tierra, reſpecto que todos los de ſu Tropa, y demas Comitiva ſe hallaban buenos, y que en ſu diviſion llevò ciento ſeſenta y tres Mulas cargadas de Proviſiones, contando aſimiſmo con el ſocorro de Viveres que havia de traer el Paquebot nombrado San Joſeph, que ſegun las diſpoſiciones, y aviſo del Illmó. Sr. Viſitador General, debia ſuponerſe navegando para el miſmo deſtino; determinó continuar ſu marcha en demanda de aquel Puerto, ſin aguardar à que la eſtacion ſe adelantaſe demaſiado, para no exponerſe à que las Nieves cerraſen el paſo de las Sierras que huvieſe en el tranſito porque ya ſe ſabia con la experiencia de aquel año, que nevaba mucho aun en San Diego, cuyas Sierras vieron nevadas á ſu arribo los que vinieron por Mar en Abril del miſmo.

En eſta inteligencia acelerò el Governador ſus diſpoſiciones, y propuſo à los dos Oficiales de Exercito D. Pedro Fages, y D. Miguel Coſtanſó de ſeguir en ſu compañia con los

los Soldados que ſe hallaſen en eſtado de hacer lo proprio, que á la ſazon eran ſeis: abrazaron dichosOficiales ſu oferta: y deſpues de haver dado parte al Excmò Señor Virrey, y al Illmò. Sr. Viſitador General de todo lo acaecido, y diſpueſto haſta entonces, el Paquebot San Antonio ſe hizo á la Vela con los Pliegos el dia nueve de Junio, con ſolos ocho Hombres de Tripulacion.

Dejóſe en San Diego la Eſcolta, que pareció ſuficiente à la Cuſtodia de la Miſion, y de los Enfermos con el Cirujano Don Pedro Prat, para que continuaſe en aſiſtirlos; dejóſe tambien competente numero de Caballada, y Mulada para ſervicio de todos: y ſe quedaron con el fin de eſtablecer aquella nueva Doctrina los Reverendos Padres Fr. Junipero Serrá, Fr. Juan Vizcayno, y Fr. Fernando Parron, aunque el primero, óbligado à ſuſpender ſu marcha por el canſancio, y fatiga paſada, quedó eſperando Embarcacion en que paſar à Monterrey, cuyo deſtino havia elegido, y los Reverendos Padres Fr. Juan Creſpi, y Fr. Juan Gomez, ſiguieron la Expedicion en ſu Viage.

Fue la ſalida de San Diego en catorce de Junio del citado año de ſeſenta y nueve: marcharon juntos los dos Trozos de la Expedicion de Tierra, diſponiendolo aſi el Comandan-

dan-

dante por fer mucho el numero de Caballada, y cargas, pues folo de Provifiones, y Viveres fe llevaron ciento, que eftimò necefarias para racionar á toda la Gente, durante feis
mefes, previniendo de efta fuerte la tardanza
de los Paquebots, aunque fe tenia por impofible que en efte intermedio dejara de llegar
alguno de ellos â Monterrey.

Obfervabafe en las marchas el Orden
figuiente: iba en la cabeza el Comandante con
los Oficiales, los feis Hombres de los voluntarios de Cataluña, que fe agregaron en San
Diego, y algunos Indios Amigos, con palas,
azadones, barras, hachas, y otros inftrumen-
tos de Gaftadores, para defmontar, y abrir
pafo fiempre que fe ofrecia: feguiafe defpues
la Requa dividida en quatro Atajos, con fus
Harrieros, y competente numero de Soldados
de Prefidio para fu Efcolta en cada uno: venia en la Retaguardia con el refto de la Tropa, é Indios Amigos el Capitan Don Fernando Rivera, comboyando la Caballada, y Mulada de remuda.

Los Soldados del Prefidio de Californias,
de quienes la jufticia, y la equidad nos obligan
à decir, que trabajaron infinito en efta Expedicion, ufan de dos generos de armas, ofenfi-
vas, y defenfivas: las defenfivas fon la Cuera,

y

y la Adarga; la primera cuya hechura es seme-
jante á la de una Casaca sin mangas, se compo-
ne de seis, ò siete azes de pieles blancas de Venado agamuzadas, impenetrable à las flechas
de los Indios, como no estén disparadas de muy
cerca. La Adarga es de dos hazes de cuero de
Toro crudo, se maneja con el brazo izquierdo,
y desvian con ella las jaras, ó flechas, defen-
diendose el Ginete à sí, y à su Caballo: usan
ademas de las dichas una especie de delantal
de baqueta prendido à la cabeza de la silla con
cayda à uno, y otro lado, que llaman armas,
ó defensas, que les cubren los muslos, y pier-
nas para no lastimarse, corriendo en el Monte:
sus armas ofensivas son la lanza, que manejan
diestramente á Caballo, la espada ancha, y una
Escopeta corta que llevan metida, y afianzada
en su funda. Son Hombres de mucho aguante,
y sufrimiento en la fatiga; obedientes, resuel-
tos, agiles, y no dificultamos decir, que son
los mayores Ginetes del Mundo, y de aquellos
Soldados que mejor ganan el Pan al Augusto
Monarca à quien sirven.

Bien se considera que las marchas de
esta Tropa con tanto Trén, y embarazos por
Tierras desconocidas, y caminos desusados, no
podian ser largas; prescindiendo de otra causa
que obligaba à hacer alto, y campar tempra-

no

no: es á decir la necefidad de explorar el terreno de un dia para otro, à fin de regularlas fobre la diftancia de los aguajes, y tomar á confequencia las precauciones convenientes, faliendo en ocafiones de parte de tarde defpues de dar agua á las Beftias en aquella mifma hora, con el informe feguro de que en el tranfito figuiente, no la havia, ó era corto el aguaje, ò efcafo el Pafto.

Los defcanfos fe median con la necefidad de quatro en quatro dias mas, ó menos, fegun la fatiga extraordinaria, ocafionada por mayor afpereza del camino, trabajo de los Gaftadores, ó extravio de las Beftias, que fe echaban menos en la Caballada, y era forzofo bufcar por fu raftro: otras vezes por la necefidad de contemporizar con los Enfermos, quando los huvo que con el tiempo fueron muchos, que á la continuada fatiga, á los excefivos calores, y frios crueles rindieron fus fuerzas.

Pero el mayor riefgo de eftos Viages, y el enemigo mas temible, es la mifma Caballada, fin la qual, no pueden tampoco lograrfe: afombranfe de noche eftos Animales en Pais que no conocen con increible facilidad: baftales para dar eftampida (fegun terminos de efta Tierra) el defcubrir á un Coyote, ò Zorra: un Pajaro que pafa volando, el polvo que el vien-

to arroja fon capazes de efpantarlos, y hacer-
los correr muchas leguas, precipitandofe por
Barrancas, y Defpeñaderos, fin que valga hu-
mana diligencia para contenerlos: cuefta defpues inmenfo trabajo el recogerlos, lo que no
es azequible fiempre; y los que no murieron
defpeñados, ò fe eftropearon en fu impetuofa
carrera, quedan de ningun fervicio en mucho
tiempo; pero no experimentò atrazo confide-
rable èfta Expedicion, por femejante acafo,
mediante el cuidado, y la vigilancia que fe ob-
fervó fiempre; pues aunque en algunas ocafiones dieron los Animales eftampida, no fe figuiò
defgracia, ò perjuicio alguno, porque fue de
corta duracion.

En la forma, y fegun el metodo referidos, exêcutaron los Efpañoles fus marchas,
atravefando Tierras immenfas, mas fertiles,
y mas alegres à medida que internaban mas
para el Norte: todas en general fon pobladas
de multitud de Indios, que falian à recibirlos,
y en partes los acompañaban de un tranfito à
otro; Gente muy docil, y manfa, mayormente
de San Diego en adelante.

Los Indios en quienes fe reconoció mas
viveza, é induftria, fon los que habitan las Iflas, y la Cofta de la Canal de Santa Barbara: viven en Pueblos, cuyas Cafas de forma esferica

á modo de una media Naranja, cubiertas de Enea, tienen hafta veinte varas de diametro: contiene cada Cafa tres, ó quatro Familias: el Hogar eftá en medio: y en la parte fuperior de la Cafa dejan refpiradero, ó chimenea para dar falida al humo. En nada defmintieron eftos Gentiles la afabilidad, y buen trato que experimentaron en otro tiempo los Efpañoles que abordaron á eftas Coftas con el General Sebaftian Vizcayno. Son de buen talle, y afpecto Hombres, y Mugeres, muy amigos de pintarfe, y embijarfe la cara, y el cuerpo: ufan grandes penachos de plumas, y unas banderillas que fujetan entre los cabellos, con diferentes dijes, y avalorios de Coral de varios colores. Los Hombres van enteramente defnudos, pero gaftan en tiempo de frio unas capas largas de pieles de Nutria curtidas, y unos mantos hechos de las proprias pieles, cortadas en tiras largas, que tuercen de manera, que todo el pelo queda por defuera; tejen luego eftos hilos unos con otros, formando trama, y les dan el corte referido.

Las Mugeres van con mas honeftidad, ceñida la cintura con pieles de Venado curtido, que las cubren por delante, y por detras hafta mas de media pierna, con un capotillo de Nutria fobre el cuerpo: las hay de buenas

fac-

facciones; ellas ſon las que tejen las batéas, y
vaſijas de junco, á las quales dan mil formas
diferentes, y figuras gracioſas, ſegun los uſos
à que las deſtinan, ya ſea para comer, beber,
guardar ſus Semillas, ú otros fines, porque no
conocen eſtas Gentes el uſo del barro, como
lo uſan las de San Diego.

Los Hombres labran hermoſas batéas
de madera, con embutidos firmes de coral, ó
de hueſo, y unos vaſos de mucha capacidad
cerrados de boca, que parecen hechos al tor-
no, y que con eſta maquina no ſaldrian mas
bien vaciados, ni de forma mas perfeſta: dan
al todo un luſtre, que parece obra acabada de
mano de Artifice havil. Las vaſijas grandes
que contienen el Agua ſon de un tejido muy
robuſto de juncos embreados por dentro, y les
dan la miſma figura que á nueſtras tinajas.

Para comer las Semillas, que gaſtan en
lugar de Pan las tueſtan primero en grandes
batèas, echando entre las Semillas algunos gui-
jarros, ó chinas, caldeadas haſta quedar rojas:
mueven entonces, y menean la batéa para no
quemarla, y dejando la Semilla ſuficientemen-
te toſtada la muelen en morteros, ó almirezes
de piedra: hay de eſtos almirezes de tamaño
extraordinario, tan bien labrados como ſi para
el efeſto tuvieſen las mejores herramientas; y

K   ſon

ſon bien dignas de admiracion la conſtancia,
prolijidad, y trabajo que emplean en acabar
eſtas piezas, tan apreciables entre ellos miſmos, que à los que dejan ſemejantes obras, para que no ſe pierda la memoria de ſu habili-
dad, y aplicacion, ſuelen colocarlas deſpues de
ſu muerte encima del paraje donde fueron ſe-
pultados.

Entierran á los muertos, tienen ſus Ce-
menterios dentro del miſmo Pueblo: los fune-
rales de ſus Capitanes ſe hazen con mucha
pompa, y colocan ſobre ſus cuerpos unas varas, ó perchas ſumamente altas de que cuel-
gan variedad de utiles, y muebles, que eran de
ſu uſo: ponen tambien en el miſmo paraje
unas grandes tablas de Pino con diferentes pin-
turas, y figuras en que explicarán ſin duda las
hazañas, y proezas del Perſonage.

No es licita la pluralidad de Mugeres
entre eſtas Gentes, ſolo los Capitanes tienen
derecho de caſar con dos. En todos ſus Pueblos ſe puſo reparo en una eſpecie de Hombres, que vivian como las Mugeres, ſe acompañaban con ellas, veſtian el miſmo traje, ſe
adornaban con avalorios, pendientes, gargan-
tillas, y otros adornos Mugeriles, y lograban
de grande conſideracion entre ellos. La falta
de Interprete, no permitió averiguar, que cla-
ſe

se de Hombres eran, ni á que Minifterio fe deftinaban, aunque todos recelaron defecto en el fexo, ò algun abufo entre aquellos Gentiles.

En fus Cafas tienen los Matrimonios fus camas feparadas en tarimas levantadas del fuelo: fus colchones fon unos fimples Petates, ò Efteras de Enea, y fus almohadas fon de lo mifmo, arrollados los Petates en la cabezera: todas eftas camas eftan colgadas con iguales Efteras, que firven à la decencia, y defienden del frio.

Sobrefale la deftreza, y havilidad de eftos Indios en la conftruccion de fus Lanchas hechas de tablazon de Pino: tienen de ocho á diez varas de largo comprehendido fu lanzamiento, y vara, y media de manga: no entra en fu fabrica hierro alguno, cuyo ufo conocen poco; pero fujetan las tablas con firmeza unas con otras, labrando de trecho à trecho fus barrenos, à diftancia de una pulgada del canto, correfpondientes unos á otros en las tablas fuperiores, y en las inferiores, y por eftos barrenos pafan fuertes ligaduras de nervios de Venado: embrean, y calafatean las cofturas, y pintan el todo de viftofas colores; manejanlas con igual maña, y falen Mar afuera á pefcar en ellas, tres, ó quatro Hombres, fiendo capa-

zes

zes de cargar hasta ocho, ò diez: usan remos largos de dos palas, y vogan con indecible lijereza, y velocidad: conocen todas las artes de pescar, y abunda el Pescado sobre sus Costas, como se dixo de San Diego. Tienen comunicacion, y Comercio con los Naturales de las Islas, de donde sacan los avalorios de coral, que corren en vez de moneda por todas estas Tierras: aunque tienen en mas estimacion los avalorios de vidrio, que les daban los Españoles, ofreciendoles quanto poseen en cambio de ellos, como son batéas, pieles de Nutria, xicaras, y platos de madera; aprecian mas que todo qualesquiera navaja, é instrumento cortante, cuyas ventajas, sobre los de pedernal, admiran: causandoles mucha satisfaccion el vér hacer uso de las hachas, y machetes, y la facilidad con que los Soldados para hacer leña derrivahā un Arbol con dichos Instrumentos.

Son asimismo grandes Cazadores: para matar á los Venados, y Verrendos, se valen de una industria admirable: conservan el cuero de la cabeza, y parte del pescuezo de alguno de estos Animales, desollado con cuidado, dejandole sus llaves pegadas al mismo cuero, que rellenaron de sacáte, ó paja para conservarle su forma: aplicanse dicha armazon como gorro

so-

sobre la cabeza, y salen al Monte con este raro equipaje: en avistando al Venado, ò Verrendo van arrastrandose poco á poco con la mano izquierda en Tierra: en la derecha llevan el arco con quatro flechas: bajan, y levantan la cabeza, moviendola á un lado, y otro, y haciendo otras demonstraciones tan proprias de estos Animales, que los atraen sin dificultad al lazo, y al tenerlos á corta distancia, les disparan sus flechas á golpe seguro.

Vieronse entre ellos algunos pedazos de Espada ancha, fierro, y fragmentos de plata labrada, que siendo de poca monta, hicieron novedad à nuestra Gente; y preguntados por señas, como adquirian aquellas cosas, señalaban, que de la Tierra adentro azia Levante; y aunque el Nuevo Mexico se halla muy distante por aquel Rumbo, es factible, que de mano en mano, con el tiempo hayan llegado á su poder dichas alhajas.

Su Lengua es sonora, y de facil pronunciacion: creyeron algunos hallarle cierta conexion con la Mexicana en la que, la L, y T. suenan frequentemente, como se reparò entre estos Naturales: pero los que poseen el Mexicano, podràn mejor inferirlo por las siguientes vozes.

Vozes de dicha Lengua.	*Su valor en la Española.*
Nucchù	La Cabeza,
Kejuhé	El Pecho.
Huachajá	La Mano.
Chipucú	El Codo.
Tocholò	El Sobaco.
Tononomò	El Muslo.
Pistocù	La Rodilla.
Kippejuè	La Pierna.
Acteme	El Pie.
Tomol	Lancha, ò Canoa.
Apa	Rancheria.
Temí	Capitan, òPrincipal.
Amo.	No.

Vozes Numericas.

Pacà	Uno.
Excò	Dos.
Maseja	Tres.
Scumu	Quatro.
Itipaca	Cinco.
Itixco	Seis.
Itimasge	Siete.
Malahua	Ocho.
Upax	Nueve.
Kerxco	Diez.

De

De la Canal de Santa Barbara en adelante, las Tierras no fon tan pobladas, ni los Indios tan induftriofos, pero fon igualmente afables, y manfos. Siguieron los Efpañoles fu Viage fin opoficion hafta la Sierra de Santa Lucia, que configuieron pafar con mucho trabajo: à la caída de dicha Sierra de la vanda del Norte, fe halla el Puerto de Monterrey, fegun relaciones antiguas, entre las Puntas de Pinos, y de Año nuevo. Dieron vifta los Efpañoles à dichas Puntas en primero de Octubre del año de fefenta y nueve, y creyendo haver llegado al termino de fu Viage defpachó el Comandante los Exploradores para reconocer la de Pinos: en cuyas immediaciones yace dicho Puerto por treinta y feis grados, quarenta minutos de latitud Boreal. Pero las feñas efcafas, y equivocas que de él refiere el Piloto Cabrera Bueno, unico Norte de efte Viage, y la naturaleza de efte Puerto, que mas antes merece el nombre de Bahía, fiendo efpaciofa (à femejanza de la de Cadiz) no confrontando con la idea, que es natural formarfe, leyendo los Derroteros del referido Cabrera Bueno, ni con la latitud de treinta y fiete grados, bajo la qual lo fitúa; fe perfuadieron los Exploradores à que el Puerto eftaria mas al Norte, y volbieron al Campo, que ocupaban los nueftros, con

L 2

no-

noticia de que no parecia en aquellos parages lo que fe bufcaba.

Contabanfe à la fazon Enfermos, hafta diez, y fiete Hombres, tullidos del Efcorbuto: la eftacion eftaba adelantada, los trabajos de cuftodiar, y velar la Caballada, cargar la Requa, los Guardias del Real, y fobre todo los reconocimientos, y exploraciones del terreno pedian, por fer naturalmente pefados, mayor numero de Gente, que la que havia en eftado de hacer efte fervicio; de fuerte, que el Comandante, hallandofe dudofo en el partido que mas convendria abrazar entre aguardar en aquel parage á que pareciefe algun Barco, ó feguir la marcha en bufca del Puerto de Monterrey, en que confideraba las dificultades, que van expueftas, no atreviendofe à refolver por si en efte afunto, llamó à Confejo á fus Oficiales, que unanimes con él fueron de fentir, que fe figuiefe la marcha, pues de no llegar al Puerto, y Paradero de los Barcos para entregarfe de los Viveres utiles, y Municiones necefarias al Eftablecimiento, que debia hacerfe en Monterrey, no debian prometerfe el focorro que tanto necefitaban, ni era pofible formar el Eftablecimiento que fe havia mandado; y que por ultimo convenia mas pafar en bufca del Puerto, que no havia de eftar lejos, fegun

gun toda evidencia, que tomar defde luego un partido, que fiempre fe eftaba à tiempo de elegir, en cafo que fuefen à peor los Enfermos, ó fe aumentafe el numero de ellos.

Refolviófe pues, profeguir el Viage, volviendo en efta ocafion la efpalda al Puerto que fe bufcaba. Los Enfermos padecieron mucho en efta marcha: vieronfe algunos à toda extremidad, lo que retardaba notablemente la marcha, fiendo precifo hacer defcanzo á cada tranfito; empezaron en efte tiempo (á fines de Octubre) las Aguas, y con ellas entró una Epidemia de diarrea, que fe comunicó à todos fin excepcion, y fe llegó à temer, que efta Enfermedad, que poftraba las fuerzas, y dejaba á los Sugetos exanimes, no acabafe enteramente con la Expedicion; pero fucedió muy al contrario, porque quantos adolecian, y padecian del Efcorbuto, tullidos, hinchados de todos fus miembros, y cargados de dolores, empezaron defde entonces á experimentar alivio en fus males: difiparonfe poco à poco las hinchazones, cefaron los dolores, recobraron el ufo de fus miembros, y por ultimo fu perfecta falud, fin medicamento alguno.

El dia ultimo de Octubre llegó la Expedicion de Tierra à vifta de la Punta de los Reyes, y Farallones del Puerto de San Francif-

M   co,

co, cuyas feñas confrontadas con las que refiere el Derrotero del Piloto Cabrera Bueno, fe
hallaron exactas. Entonces fe vino en eviden-
te conocimiento de que el Puerto de Monterrey fe havia dexado atrás, fiendo pocos los
que duraban en la opinion contraria: fin embargo el Comandante refolviò embiar á reconocer el Terreno hafta la Punta de los Reyes;
los Exploradores que fueron Comifionados para el efecto fe vieron atajados por immenfos
Efteros, que fe internan extraordinariamente
en la Tierra, y precifaban á dar grandes ro-
deos para defcabezarlos: emplearon tres dias
en efte reconocimiento, y volbieron diciendo,
que fegun las feñas que les dieron los Indios,
no podian dudar que el Puerto dejafe de eftar
muy cerca, y que feguramente havia llegado
alguno de los Paquebots, que creian fer el San
Jofeph à fu deftino: hizòfe poco aprecio de efta
noticia adquirida por el equivoco medio de
feñas de manos, y cabeza, que en femejantes
ocafiones ufurpan el oficio de la lengua; fin
embargo para no retirarfe con efte efcrupulo,
fe refolviò pafar adelante, hafta cerciorarfe del
hecho: llegados al remate del primer Eftero,
y reconocido el Terreno, que fe havia de feguir para llegar á la Punta de los Reyes, inter-
rumpido con nuevos Efteros, efcafo de Paftos,

y

y de Leña, haviendoſe conocido á demas de eſto lo incierto de la noticia, y la equivocacion que padecieron los Exploradores. El Comante, con parecer de ſus Oficiales, reſolvió la retirada azia la Punta de Pinos, con eſperanzas de hallar al Puerto de Monterrey, y encontrar en el, al Paquebot el San Joſeph, ó el San Antonio, cuyo ſocorro ſe hacia ya neceſario, pues de las Proviſiones que ſe tomaron en San Diego, no quedaban mas que unos quantos coſtales de Harina de que ſe les ſubminiſtraba à cada individuo una corta Racion diaria. Con la Polvora, y el Plomo ſe ſuplia en algo la falta de las demas coſas, porque era abundante la caza, ſobre todo la de Anzares, y Patos, que en tiempo de Invierno abundan extraordinariamente por aquella Tierra.

El dia once de Noviembre ſe puſo en execucion la retirada en demanda de Monterrey: los Eſpañoles llegaron à dicho Puerto, y Punta de Pinos en veinte, y ocho de Noviembre: mantuvieronſe en eſte Sitio haſta el dia diez de Diciembre, ſin que en eſte tiempo huvieſe parecido Embarcacion alguna, por cuyo motivo viendoſe aſimiſmo faltos de Viveres, y que la Sierra de Santa Lucia iba cubriendoſe de Nieve, el Comandante D. Gaſpar de Portolá ſe vió obligado à tomar el partido

tido de continuar la retirada haſta San Diego, dejando para mejor ocaſion el bolver á la Empreſa.

Experimentaron los Eſpañoles en eſta retirada algunos trabajos, y neceſidades, porque faltaron enteramente las Proviſiones, y que las largas marchas, que la neceſidad obligaba hacer para llegar á San Diego, no daban tiempo á buſcar el ſuſtento en la caza, ni eſta abundaba igualmente en todas partes: mataronſe en eſta ocaſion doze Mulas de la Requa, de cuya carne ſe alimentò la Gente haſta San Diego, á cuyo nuevo Eſtablecimiento llegaron todos con ſalud en veinte y quatro de Enero de mil ſetecientos ſetenta.

Hallaronſe en buen eſtado ſus humildes Fabricas, cercadas de palizada de troncos de Arboles, capaz de buena defenſa en caſo neceſario: recobrados de la fatal Epidemia del Eſcorbuto á muchos de los Soldados, y Marineros que quedaron Enfermos en el año antecedente, aunque el mayor numero de ellos, y eran los que primero havian contrahido el contagio en la Mar, murieron irremediablemente.

Los Reverendos Padres Miſioneros eſtaban convaleciendo de la comun Enfermedad, como tambien el Cirujano Don Pedro Prat,

Prat, y Don Vicente Vila, porque el contagio
no perdonò á perſona alguna de los que en eſta
Expedicion fueron comprehendidos.

Havia en San Diego Proviſiones de
Mayz, Harina, y Semillas ſuficiente à la ma-
nutencion de los que componian el Preſidio
para algunos Meſes, pero con la venida de ſeſenta Hueſpedes, no podia contarſe que dura-
ſen mucho tiempo, y era de temer que ſi los
Barcos tardaſen en traher el Socorro ſobre que
ſe contaba, no ſe vieſen aquellos Eſpañoles
obligados de la hambre a abandonar enteramente una Conquiſta, que aun ſiendo muy fe-
liz havia coſtado tantos ſudores, y tantas vi-
das: mas para no exponerſe á tal deſcredito,
diſpuſo el Comandante, que el Capitan del
Preſidio de Californias con quarenta Hombres
ſiguieſe la Marcha haſta aquella Peninſula, con
el fin de acopiar en ſus Miſiones los Viveres
que pudieſe, y traer el Ganado en pie, que ſegun ſe dijo al principio havia quedado en Ve-
licatà, y cuya flaqueza no permitiò ſiguiera la
Marcha: acertada providencia, en que ſe mi-
raba á la actual conſervacion de lo adquirido,
diſminuyendo el crecido numero de conſu-
midores de los Viveres que havia exiſtentes,
y à los medios de hacerles ſubſiſtir en lo ſuc-
ceſivo, aun quando faltaſen los Socorros Ma-
riti-

N

ritimos, tan importantes para llevar à debido efecto la defeada Emprefa de Monterrey.

Salió efte Deftacamento, con el objeto dicho en diez de Febrero de mil fetecientos fetenta. Y por efte medio fe diò nuevamente cuenta al Excmò. Sr. Virrey, è Illmó. Sr. Vifitador General del eftado de las cofas, lo acaecido, vifto, y defcubierto hafta entonces por aquellos Efpañoles en fu dilatado Viage de la California Septentrional, en donde los que quedaban efperando las Ordenes de dichos Superiores tardaron poco en recibir el confuelo que pedia el trifte eftado à que fe veian reducidos.

El dia veinte, y tres de Marzo llegò, y diò fondo en el Puerto de San Diego el Paquebot de Su Mageftad el San Antonio al mando de fu Capitan, y Piloto D Juan Perez; haviafe hecho à Vela de San Blas en veinte de Diciembre del año pafado de mil fetecientos fefenta, y nueve, experimentó en fu Viage recios temporales, y vientos contrarios, que lo hecharon á quatrocientas leguas de la Cofta, y haviendofe vifto precifado volber en demanda de efta para hacer agua, tomó Tierra por treinta, y cinco grados de Latitud, defde donde prefentando la Proa al Sur, y el coftado izquierdo á la Cofta en bufca de algun Surgidero,

arri-

arribò à la Punta de la Concepcion por treinta, y quatro grados, y medio de Latitud Norte; Tierra la mas Occidental de la Canal de
Santa Barbara, à cuyo abrigo configuiò hacer
fu aguada junto à una Poblacion de Gentiles,
quienes le dieron razon individual de la Expedicion de Tierra, declarando por feñas nada
equivocas, como havian pafado los Eftrangeros yendo para el Norte, y bolvieron defpues
á pafar faltos de comida, tirando para el Sur,
montados en fus Caballos, lo que exprefaban
poniendofe en femejante poftura fobre los
barriles, que los Marineros echaban en Tierra, y haciendo otras demonftraciones proprias
de un Hombre á Caballo. Referian afimifmo
los nombres de varios Soldados, que como
fuefen conocidos de algunos de los Marineros, fe echó de ver, que no fonaban á cafuales
aquellas vozes.

Convencido Perez de que la Expedicion de Tierra fe havia retirado, en lo que no
admitió duda, porque no ignoraba, que los
Viveres no podian haverles durado hafta entonces, determinò arribar à San Diego para
fubminiftrarles lo que necefitafen á fin de fa-
cilitar fu Viage la vuelta de Monterrey fu
deftino.

Efte era el partido que convenia tomar,
y

y tomó en efecto el Comandante D. Gaspar de Portolá, sin embargo de hallarse con poca Tropa para emprender segunda vez una marcha tan dilatada; pero el conocimiento que tenia de la buena indole de los Naturales de aquellas Tierras, y la Hospitalidad que tan exactamente, y en todas partes havian observado con los Españoles en su primera entrada, quitó en esta ocasion todo recelo, y desconfianza; fue resuelta la marcha, y tomando las Provisiones necesarias se puso por obra en diez y siete de Abril del corriente año, con solos veinte Hombres entre Soldados Presidiarios, y Voluntarios de Cataluña con su Oficial D. Pedro Fages.

El Ingeniero D. Miguel Costansó, conforme á las Ordenes con que se hallaba se embarcò en el Paquebot el San Antonio, á cuyo bordo se transfirió tambien el Reverendisimo Padre Presidente Fr. Junipero Serrá, y se hizo á la Mar esta Embarcacion en diez y seis de Abril del proprio año.

Llegaron todos á Monterrey, los de Tierra en veinte y tres de Mayo; y el San Antonio en treinta y uno del dicho arrojò sus anclas en el mismo Puerto, y Fondeadero, en donde ciento sesenta y ocho años antes estuvo Surta la Esquadra del General Vizcayno, no, embiada por el Conde de Monterrey al Deſcubrimiento de eſtas Coſtas, de Orden del Señor Don Felipe Tercero. Hallaſe eſte Puerto conforme ſe dixo, por treinta y ſeis grados, y quarenta minutos de latitud Septentrional, á la cayda de la Sierra de Santa Lucia de la parte del Norte de ella. Su principal abrigo es la Punta de Pinos tendida (no de Nordeſte Sudoeſte conforme la ſitúa el Piloto Cabrera Bueno) ſino de Norueſte Sueſte, y de la vanda del Nordeſte de ella, ſe halla el Surgidero en que puede anclar qualeſquiera Embarcacion por quatro, ſeis, ocho brazadas fondo de Arena menuda, buen tenedero, ſegun eſtuviere mas, ò menos inmediata a Tierra.

La Punta de Pinos que defiende el Surgidero del Norueſte eſtá toda ceñida de piedras, y de cantiles, pero deſpues de las piedras entra una hermoſa Playa bordada de Meganos la vuelta del Eſte, girando luego al Nordeſte, y Norte haſta un Eſtero muy grande con diferentes brazos, diſtante del principio de la Playa dicha, mas de tres leguas: ſigue deſpues la Coſta bolviendo al Norueſte, y Oeſte de Tierra algo grueſa veſtida de Arboleda acantilada en partes, haſta la Punta de Año nuevo que muere en la Mar por treinta, y ſiete grados, y tres minutos de Latitud quedando el Surgidero rodea-

O

deado de la Tierra por todas partes, menos
del Nornorueste por donde unicamente ca-
rece de abrigo.

La Tierra que regiſtra eſta inmenſa Bahía viſta deſde la Mar, forma una agradable
perſpectiva, porque mirando para el Sur ſe
deja vér la Sierra de Santa Lucia, que deſpi-
diendo de ſí unas lomas mas bajas à proporcion que ſe arriman à la Playa, coronadas ſus
cumbres de Pinos, y cubiertas de Paſtos pre-
ſentan un magnifico amfiteatro, que ſe hace
mas viſtoſo con el verdor de diferentes Cañadas que interrumpen el terreno, y cauſan admirable variedad, y harmonia à los ojos. No
tiene agua corriente eſte Puerto, pero ſe halla
la ſuficiente en una ondonada, ó bajial al Sueſte
del deſembarcadero, que es donde principia la
Playa, en cuyo Parage ſe paſa á ſeco un Eſtero, que ſe llena ſolamente en mareas vivas, y
ſe interna baſtante hazia el Eſte. Eſte bajial es
muy humedo, y por tanto crece mucha yerva
en èl, y ſiempre ſe mantiene verde: cabando
pues en qualquiera parte, y abriendo pozos,
ſe hallará agua dulce, y buena caſi al pelo de
la Tierra; y ſerá mejor ſi ſe quiere practicar
eſta diligencia un poco mas adentro en alguna Cañadita de las muchas que alli vienen à
deſembocar, pues en ellas ſe deſcubrieron varios

rios manantiales, aunque cortos de excelente agua.

De la vanda del Nordeſte, y del Eſte, ſe eſtiende el Pais en hermoſas llanuras, que termínan en la Sierra con varias Lagunitas, aunque las mas ſon de Agua ſalóbre, en algunas ſe quaja mucha ſal; el terreno en general es areniſco, pero hay muchos bajiales de excelente migajon: y al Sur del Puerto, à diſtancia de dos leguas cortas hay una Cañada eſpacioſa, por la qual baja el Rio llamado del Carmelo, donde hay unos Sacatáles, ó Pajonales, que cubren enteramente à un Hombre à Caballo, prueba de la feracidad del terreno; ſus producciones ſon apreciables, porque hay Nogales, Avellanos, y Cerezos, como en Europa: Zarzamora, Roſales, Yerva buena en todas partes.

En la Sierra hay Robles, y Encinos corpulentiſimos, que producen buena Bellota, Pinos, que crian Piñas, y Piñones en abundancia: Boſques de Sabinos, de Cipreſes, y otros varios Palos.

Los Naturales de Monterrey viven en la Sierra: los mas cercanos à la Playa diſtan de ella como legua, y media, bajan à vezes, y ſalen á peſcar en Balzitas de Enea, pero no debe ſer la peſca ſu principal mantenimiento, y ſo-

lo

lo recurrirán á ella quando les ayudare poco la caza, que abunda mucho en lo interior de la Sierra, ſobre todo la del Verrendo, y Venado. Son eſtos Serranos muy numeroſos, en extremo dociles, y manſos: nunca ſolian venir á viſitar à los Eſpañoles ſin llevarles buen regalo de caza, que comunmente ſe componia de dos, ó tres Venados, ó Verrendos, que ofrecian ſin exigir, ni ſiquiera pedir coſa alguna: ſu buena indole ha dado à los Reverendos Padres Miſioneros bien fundadas eſperanzas de Conquiſtarlos brevemente à la Fé de Chriſto.

Abunda en eſtas Coſtas el Peſcado no menos que en la Canal de Santa Barbara, y Puerto de San Diego: los Ballenatos, y Lobos Marinos ſon ſin numero, y con el tiempo podria tal vez facilitarſe la Peſca de los primeros en la miſma Bahía.

Erigióſe en aquella Tierra conforme lo mandado, un Preſidio, y Miſion con la Advocacion de San Carlos, cooperando todos con igual eſmero, y ſolicitud, Tropa, Marineria, y ſus reſpectivos Oficiales á los humildes principios de tan importante Eſtablecimiento; en el que concluidas las obras Proviſionales que ſe regularon mas preciſas para los Reverendos Padres Miſioneros, y la Tropa del Preſidio, y pro-

proyectadas las demas que debian hacerse defpues, fe Almacenó la carga del Paquebot, y fe
tomó la refolucion por el Comandante Don
Gafpar de Portolá de embarcarfe en èl con el
Ingeniero Don Miguel Coftanfó, dejando el
mando al Theniente de Infanteria Don Pedro
Fages, fegun le eftaba prevenido en fus Inf-
trucciones; y para ayudar à la Tropa en fus
trabajos quedaron nueve Marineros de re-
fuerzo en Monterrey.

Salió el San Antonio de aquel Puerto el
nueve de Julio de efte año, llegó felizmente al
de San Blas el primero de Agofto; y haviendo
arribado defpues al mifmo el otro Paquebot
San Carlos, que bolviò defde San Diego, fe
difponen ambos à emprender nuevo Viage
en el proximo mes de Noviembre para conducir feparados por el Golfo interior de Californias, y por el Mar del Sur treinta Mifioneros Apoftolicos con abundantes repueftos de
Provifiones, Ropas, Utiles, y Ornamentos, à
fin de fobftener los nuevos Prefidios de San
Diego, y Monterrey con fus refpectivas Mifiones, y erigir otras en los fertiles Paifes, que
tranfitò la Expedicion de Tierra defde Velicatá hafta el Puerto de San Francifco, fituado
á los treinta y fiete grados, quarenta y cinco
minutos de Latitud.

P   Afi

Aſi han tenido ſus felizes principios los deſeados Eſtablecimientos de San Diego, y Monterrey, y aſi debemos tambien prometernos que ſe verificaràn los de las nuevas Miſiones que van à fundarſe, y crecer bajo la proteccion, y auſpicios del Excmó. Sr. Marqués de Croix, Virrey, Governador, y Capitan General de eſte dilatado Imperio, à cuyo ſuave Mando aplauden los Súbditos, y viven agradecidos los Pueblos. Pero eſta Empreſa deſeada por tantos años, y promovida muchas vezes con grandes preparativos, y gaſtos, ſerà ſin duda muy grata al Monarca Auguſto que ciñe la Corona de Eſpaña, cuyo magnanimo Corazon, y religioſa Piedad premia el Cielo con ſubſiſtar en ſu glorioſo Reynado Hombres Iluſtres, y Grandes en todos eſtados Ecleſiaſtico, Militar, y Politico que compiten igualmente en deſempeñar los altos Cargos que fia à ſu eminente capacidad, y talentos, nunca mejor empleados que en procurar la Propagacion del Evangelio, y la felicidad publica de ſus Leales, y Amantes Vaſallos.

Mexico, y Octubre 24, de 1770.

D. *Miguel Coſtanſó.*

HISTORICAL DIARY
of the Voyages by Sea and Expeditions by Land
made to the North of California
by Order
of His Excellency
MARQUES DE CROIX
Viceroy, Governor, and Captain-General
of New Spain
and by Direction
of His Most Illustrious Señor
DON JOSEPH DE GÁLVEZ
of the Council and Court of his Majesty, in the Supreme Council
of the Indies, Quartermaster General, Visitador-General
of this Kingdom.
Carried out by the Troops destined for said purpose under the command
OF DON GASPAR DE PORTOLÁ
Captain of Dragoons in the Regiment of Spain, and Governor
in said Peninsula.
And by the Packetboats the *San Carlos* and the *San Antonio,*
under the command of
DON VICENTE VILA,
Pilot of the first-class in the Royal Navy,
And of **DON JUAN PEREZ,**
of the Navigation of the Phillippines.
BY ORDER OF HIS MOST EXCELLENT SEÑOR VICEROY,
At the imprint of the Supreme Government

The Supreme Government of Spain, well-aware of the repeated attempts of a foreign nation upon the northern coasts of California, with unfavorable aims toward the Monarchy and its interests, the KING ordered the Marqués de Croix, his Viceroy and Captain-General in New Spain to take effective measures to defend that part of His Dominions from all invasion or sudden attack.

The Marqués de Croix had anticipated the plan of the Monarch in this matter, since before receiving this order, and at the time of the Expulsion of the Jesuits from New Spain, he had appointed a Political and Military Governor of California in order to carry out the same action in that Province, maintain its obedience to the Sovereign, keep the peace, and give notice of whatever event might occur.

Equally, His Excellency had resolved to send to said Peninsula intelligent persons who, devoted solely to examining carefully and looking over the discovered part of it, should inform him of the state of its Missions, of the distribution, kind, and number of its natives, their mode of living and customs, the suitable products of that land, the nature of the mines, the method which was being followed in their work, what persons were making use of them, what settlements of Spaniards or people of other races had been established, and finally of the character and nature of its coasts, harbors, and seas, in order to be able to give, in view of these accounts and of previous information, the orders and foresight conducive to the development and regulation of the commerce, mining, and settlement of those regions.

While His Excellency recognized the necessity of those reports in order to proceed with good judgement in the execution of his plans, there was also an uncertain difficulty in appointing persons who should have the qualities which such a Commission would require for its fulfillment. When impelled by the very zeal which animated His Excellency, the Most Illustrious Señor Don Joseph de Gálvez lifted the burden of this difficulty. Destined to visit the Provinces of Sinaloa and Sonora, Gálvez offered to go personally to the Californias with the desire of completing such important ideas, and putting into execution some projects whose subject matter he considered of the greatest importance.

His Excellency praised and accepted the generous offer of the Most Illustrious Señor Gálvez, and gave him the necessary delegated powers, as much to do with the Military as with Political affairs, to the end that, by himself, according to the needs and events he might apply to those affairs timely measures and regulations. The Señor Visitador-General arranged for his voyage, and set forth from Mexico City, April 9, 1768.

By May of the same year His Illustrious Lordship had arrived at the shipyard and settlement of the Port of San Blas, newly-built on the coast of New Galicia, on the South Sea, where they had built the vessels intended for the navigation and commerce with Sonora. At the same time other ships were being constructed, which should, according to the intent of this Government, serve for communication and trade with California.

While moving down to this port with the object of embarking for that Peninsula (of Baja California), His Illustrious Lordship was overtaken and handed some sealed letters from Mexico City, in which the Señor Viceroy included the order which he had recently received from the Royal Court, concerning the care and vigilance with which it was important to watch and guard the western coasts of California. His Excellency added the timely decision that the Señor Visitador should send a maritime expedition to the famous port of Monterey.

The defense and occupation of the coasts of California was one of the objects which worthily occupied the attention of the Most Excellent Señor Marqués de Croix, and with this motive he again recommended to His Illustrious Lordship a point whose importance, in his judgement, should be noted; this he added to the order of the Monarch, leaving to the prudent judgement of the Señor Visitador, the application of the means which he might judge most opportune and conducive to so praiseworthy an end.

But before relating the means employed by the Most Illustrious Señor Don Joseph de Gálvez, it is necessary to say something about the coasts of California, object of the attentions of the Government, and likewise setting forth the conditions of the Peninsula, and in general that of the trade of the South Sea, at the time of the arrival of His Illustrious Lordship at San Blas. This will make known the effectiveness of the measures, his relation to them, and to the few resources which can be related of in such remote lands.

Those northern coasts of America are known by the name of *Exteriores, ú Occidentales de la California,* or Western Coast, which bound the Asiatic Ocean, or the South Sea, and their waters run the long distance of more than 500 maritime leagues between Cape San Lucas in 22 degrees and 48 minutes north latitude, and the Río de los Reyes in 43 degrees. The Río de los Reyes is mentioned not as the limit, but as the terminus of what has been explored of these coasts by the navigators of our nation, although this is farther than has been conquered and reclaimed by the Spaniard in obedience unto their Majestic Monarch, whose Dominion is not even yet recognized by all the nations (Indian tribes) within the Peninsula. If its throat, or the part by which the Peninsula remains attached to the continent be considered as between the mouth of the Colorado River, and the Port of San Diego, two points which, with slight difference, fall under the same parallel of 32 degrees and one-half.

The narrow part of California, beginning at Cape San Lucas, is reached at thirty degrees and a half of north latitude, in which there is found the Mission of Santa María, a short distance from the Bay of San Luis Gonzaga, a very convenient and secure port upon the Sea of Cortez or Gulf of California.

But all this stretch was scarcely populated with people other than its own natives; a very few of them congregated in the Missions, and the rest scattered in different impermanent rancherias which recognized the nearest mission as the principle town. These natives whose number is fairly limited, except for their having been Catechised and made Christians, maintained in all else the same mode of seeking a livelihood as in their Gentile state: by the chase and by fishery, living in the hills to gather the seeds and fruits which the earth provides without cultivation.

The Spanish people, and other races called in America *de rázon* (civilized) and established on the Peninsula did not number 400 souls, and this includes the number of the families of the soldiers of the Presidio of Loreto and those families of several who called themselves miners, who dwelt in the region to the south. From this it can be suggested how difficult it would be to count upon the residents for the defense of these coasts, and what opportunity is offered to whatever foreigners to establish themselves thereon, without fear of finding any opposition whatever. Especially would this be so if the foreigners should have tried landing toward the north, in the celebrated Ports of San Diego and Monterey. Such an event would have brought with it fatal results for they would have been able to take possession of the land and fortify themselves in these places without (the news) coming—with the notice coming too late—to the attention of the Government, and the damage being discovered when already irremediable.

No other vessels are known upon the South Sea in all that respects the coasts of New Spain, than the packetboats recently constructed in San Blas, and two others of small tonnage which served the missionaries, who were expelled from California, for their communication with the neighboring and frontier coasts of Sonora and New Galicia. In these few ships could be found all the maritime forces which could have opposed foreign invasions.

In view, then, of the orders under which His Illustrious Lordship found himself, and of the scanty means which that Province offered; equally recognizing that it was not feasible to bring about an improvement at once, he did not desist from the obligation to which he had pledged himself. Rather, he overcame the difficulty by industry, dividing up the difficult tasks. He felt the need of peopling the discovered part of California with useful inhabitants, capable of cultivating its lands and profiting by the rich products which it offers in minerals, grain or other fruits, and likewise the taking up of arms in defense of their homes whenever the occasion should arrive. But as the regions understood as under the name California are so extensive, as has been said, it was no less necessary to advance new establishments as far as possible toward the north, which, by joining hands with those establishments of the south, should be of mutual support.

No one is ignorant of the repeated and expensive expeditions which, to realize this project and reconnoiter the Western coast of California, were made in the last two centuries. The effectiveness and success which were had by the last expedition, executed in the year 1602, by General Sebastián Vizcaíno, who managed to discover the Ports of San Diego and Monterey, the former situated in thirty-two degrees and a half north latitude, and the latter in thirty-six degrees and forty minutes. From this resulted the origination of the Royal Decree of Señor Philip Third, in which he gave orders to occupy and settle the Port of Monterey, whose usefulness was well-recognized ever since that time. He entrusted this important Commission to the same Sebastián Vizcaíno. But, although the Orders of that Monarch were given with such accord, and conceived in terms which seemed to smooth out every difficulty and to conquer all impossibilities, they were not carried out as desired—though it is not possible to say what obstacles occasioned their non-observance, though Vizcaíno died while he was arranging the enterprise.

The same political motives as in that time are present now to despatch the said orders, adding the others which have been referred to, and that prudence dictated the proper means which it was best to follow, under the real circumstances, to gain the best effectiveness.

With this view, the Most Illustrious Señor Don Joseph de Gálvez resolved, in a *Junta* over which he presided at San Blas on May 16, 1768, and there being present the Commandant of that Department, the army officers and pilots who happened to be there, to return to the enterprise with larger preparations, and occupy at once the Ports of San Diego and Monterey, establishing in them a Presidio and Mission, and with these precautions secure the possession of the land to our Majestic Sovereign against the pretension of foreign strangers. And His Illustrious Lordship reserved for a more opportune time the augmentation of those establishments to give all the solidity that is suitable.

So the maritime expedition came to be resolved, and the boats in which it was to be carried out were assigned, selecting for this purpose the *San Carlos* (alias *Toison de Oro*) and the *San Antonio* (alias *El Príncipe*) as vessels of greater tonnage and resistance. But as his Most Illustrious Lordship would have to cross to (Lower) California, in order from there to take new measures and give various orders for the same purpose, he deferred for the time the naming of officers and troops which would accompany the forces along with the Missionary Fathers who must be obtained from said Peninsula.

At that time the two packetboats were absent from San Blas, and were supposed to be navigating their way to the Port, from which they had set forth in March of that same year with a transport of troops for the Port of Guaymas, in the Province of Sonora. His Lordship left to the commandant of that Department the orders necessary for the prompt despatch and fitting out of the summoned vessels. His Lordship embarked for California on May 24 in the bilander *Sinaloa,* and on July 5, anchored in the Bay of

Cerralvo, after having personally reconnoitered the Islands of Isabela and the Marías, and the Port of Mazatlan on the coast of Sinaloa.

Meanwhile, everything necessary for so extensive and difficult a voyage was gathered together. But although the Commandant of San Blas, and the other persons charged with this important affair went ahead very solicitous against all delay, the slowness of the boats in returning to the Port, due to contrary winds, and the difficulty which for the same cause they experienced in their voyage to cross to California, delayed the maritime expedition.

The Señor Visitador-General, in the meantime, labored with tireless vigilance. And although there was more than enough in California of affairs of grave importance, worthy to occupy his attention, never did he lose sight of the projected enterprise whose successful outcome he wished to assure by as many avenues as could be tried, and by as many means as his reasoning could suggest. To His Illustrious Lordship, the maritime expedition did not appear sufficient to obtain and reach the end which he proposed. He considered the infinite risks and mishaps to which the vessels were exposed in a prolonged sailing and which might be called "new sailings," by reason of the scant information which they had, the sicknesses which assailed the crews, as frequently in long voyages, and other inevitable risks. From these considerations was born the determination to send another expedition by land, which directing itself toward the same destinations as the maritime expedition, could lend to or receive from the latter according to circumstances such assistance as they might mutually need.

To this end, His Illustrious Lordship despatched to all the Reverend Ministrant Priests of the Missions of the Peninsula a charge for each mission to contribute the effects which, without serious deprivation, could be spared, in the way of sacred vestments and sacred vessels for the new missions, dried fruits and wine, oil, or broth, for said land expeditions including horses and mules.

The provisions and food supplies for the trip by land were embarked at the Presidio of Loreto, aboard four launches manned to carry them to the Bay of San Luis Gonzaga from where they went forward toward the north, named as the point of meeting and departure. Following the road went the troops, muleteers, and vaqueros with the herd of every sort, which had to be taken by land as both cargo carriers and as stock for the projected establishments.

These troops composed of forty men of the California Company, were joined by thirty others, and Indian volunteers from the missions armed with bows and arrows. All were to have marched under the orders of the Governor of the Peninsula, Don Gaspar de Portolá, but His Lordship found it more advantageous to make two divisions of them. The Captain of the Presidio of Loreto, Don Fernando Rivera y Moncada, was to lead the first division in the capacity of Scout, with twenty-five men of his troop, and some friendly Indians, taking the cattle herd. The Governor,

Commander-in-Chief of the expedition was to follow later with the rest of the men and provisions.

The first Division was to have left, according to the orders given by His Illustrious Lordship, early in December, but the severity of the roads, the difficulty of getting the herds together, and of conducting them through lands scant of pasturage and of watering-places—as are those of the north of Lower California—considerably slowed down the march. The cattle herd which arrived at the Mission of Santa Maria in the early part of March 1769, was totally worn out for the continuing trip in such a way that it was indispensable to leave them in Velicatá to regain their strength, holding off until a better occasion arose to drive them to (Upper California) as was carried out later.

In Velicatá a new *Doctrina,* under the Advocacy of San Fernando (the Mission San Fernando de Velicatá was founded by the Franciscans in Baja California) since this stopping-place, is some twenty leagues distance from the Mission of Santa Maria, and much frequented by the Gentile Indians of the North of (Lower) California. A sufficient escort was left at this place, and from here the first division of the expedition by land pursued its march on March 24, of said year.

The second division of the expedition which the Governor led, set forth from this same stopping place of Velicatá, on May 15, carrying in its company the President of the Missions of California, the Most Reverend Father Fray Junipero Serra, in whom, at an advanced age, neither the excessive and inseparable hardships of so prolonged a trip, nor those hardships which awaited him in his longed-for Apostolate of Monterey, were enough to restrain the ardent zeal of which he lives possessed for the conversion of that infinite Heathendom to the knowledge of the true God and of His Holy Law of Grace.

The packetboats the *San Carlos* and *El Príncipe* (alias *San Antonio*) which, according to the orders of His Lordship, were to have stopped at the Port of La Paz, in southern (Lower) California, in order to set out from there with the veteran land troops, the tools, ammunition and provisions for the new establishments of San Diego and Monterey, were delayed in arriving at that port, for the cause hinted at the outset. The *San Carlos* came in at the middle of December, as it must have labored much on the sea, straining with the winds, which had weakened it, and some of the oakum had worked out from the seams, causing the vessel to leak. This was not a mishap to be neglected, and it was judged indispensable to heel her over, to show the seams and the keel—an operation which had its difficulty in a country little less than destitute of whatever was necessary for the purpose. It was effected, nevertheless; His Lordship urging it on by his presence and example; and in less than fifteen days the vessel took on all its cargo; and being ready to set sail, the troops embarked. These consisted of twenty-five men of a Company of Catalonian Volunteers, with their Lieutenant Don Pedro Fages whom His Lordship had ordered to come from the Army or Expedition of Sonora, the Engineer Don Miguel Costansó, and the Surgeon Don Pedro Prat. There embarked also, for the spiritual care of all, the very Reverend Father Fray Fernando Parrón, a Religious of the College of Propaganda Fide de San Fernando in Mexico City, who would remain in San Diego to find that Mission.

At this time news was had of the other packetboat the *San Antonio,* which, finding itself already very near the port (of La Paz) was driven to leeward by a fierce wind from the northwest, and became obliged to put into the Port of Pulmo, a stopping place and anchorage which has some shelter from said wind, on the southern coast of the Peninsula, from where its Captain Don Juan Pérez, sent advices of this occurrence. His Lordship then feared that if the Norwesters kept up their force it would not fall off more to the leeward if his pilots attempted to enter the port. Aware of this, he despatched an order to said Captain to cross the Bay of San Bernabé, situated on the Cape of San Lucas, upon this same coast, and in the most southerly part of the Peninsula, where His Lordship resolved to transfer himself in the packet *La Concepción.*

The *Concepción* and the *San Carlos* put to sea at the same time from the Port of La Paz, on January 10, 1769. They navigated in company until the 14th of the same month, on which day they entered and anchored in the Bay of San Bernabé. But as the *San Antonio* had not yet arrived, His Lordship decided to send the *San Carlos* on ahead to San Diego, and on the following day, in the afternoon, this packetboat weighed its anchors and set sail.

The *San Antonio* arrived at the designated Bay of San Bernabé in the latter part of January, and although it was in no trouble, the Señor Visitador resolved to also give it a careening to go over its seams. And having been fixed up like the *San Carlos* it put to sea with the same destination on the 15th of February.

The navigation of the California coast has an inseparable difficulty in the constancy of the north and northwest winds, which last through all the year with little interruption, and are directly opposed to the voyage. The coastline angles from northwest to southeast, which obligates every vessel to withdraw from the coast and run out to sea until it encounters winds more favorable and variable with which, running as far north as they need, they can stand in to windward of the port to which they are bound.

On this presumption, and with orders to follow the method indicated, the two packets made their voyage to the Port of San Diego, but with different fortunes. The *San Carlos* experienced such contrary winds and calms, that finding itself driven to sea more than 200 leagues from the coast, and short of water, it had to stand in to the coast to seek water. It did so on the Island of Cerros (Cedros) with great difficulty and hard work, the ship keeping under sail, tacking between land and the Island, with no shelter nor anchorage whatever where an anchor could be dropped without risk of losing it on account of the bad nature of the bottom.

Having concluded taking on water, the ship put to sea on March 26, and on April 29, entered the Port of San Diego, one hundred and ten days out of La Paz. But its crew, and the troops it transported—whose hardships could not fail to be excessive in so long and painful a voyage, and in the rawest of the winter, arrived in a deplorable state. Scurvy had infected all without exception, in such a way that on entering San Diego, two men had already died of the sickness; most of the seamen, and half of the troops found themselves prostrate in their beds. Only four sailors remained on their feet, and attended, aided by the troops, to trimming and furling the sails and other work on board ship.

The packet *San Antonio,* although it had put forth one month after the *San Carlos,* had the fortune to finish the voyage in 59 days, and had been lying in the Port of San Diego since April 11. But it had half of its crew equally affected by scurvy, of which illness two men had also died. Amid so much sickness, all showed happiness in being reunited, and with common accord, after the *San Carlos* had tied up in a convenient spot, the officers resolved to attend to the prompt alleviation of the sick.

The first business was to seek a place to get water from which to supply and fill the barrels with good water for the use of the men. For that purpose on May first, the Officers Don Pedro Fages, Don Miguel Costansó, and the second Captain of the *San Carlos,* Don Gorge Estorace, with the troops and mariners who found themselves in better shape for fatigue-duty, numbered twenty-one men. Following the west shore of the Port, they discovered a short distance away a group of Indians armed with bows and arrows, to whom they made signs with white cloths calling them to a parley. But, keeping at a distance, moving away as our men moved toward them, prevented a meeting. Nor was it possible, either, for our men to make greater speed, for they were weak, and after such a long voyage had, as it were, lost the use of their legs. These Indians stopped every little while upon some height, watching our men, and showing the fear which the strangers caused them by the very thing they did to hide it. They thrust one point of their bows down in the soil, and grasping it by the other end they danced and whirled about with indescribable velocity. But, as soon as they saw our men draw near, they again withdrew themselves with the same swiftness. At last it was contrived to attract them by sending toward them one soldier, who, depositing his arms on the earth, and using gestures and signs of peace, they consented to let him near. He distributed some gifts to them while the others were coming up, who finished assuring these Gentiles with some more considerable presents of ribbons, glass, beads, and baubles. They asked them by signs where the watering-place was, and the natives, pointing toward a grove which was made out in the distance to the northeast, gave to understand that within it ran some river or arroyo, and to follow, that they would take them to it.

They walked some three leagues, until they arrived on the banks of a river hemmed in on either bank by a low ridge of very leafy willows and cottonwoods. Its channel must have been twenty varas wide, and it discharges into an estuary which at high tide could admit the launch, and make it convenient for accomplishing the taking on of water. Within the grove was a variety of shrubs and odoriferous plants, as the Rosemary, the Sage, Roses of Castile, and above all a quantity of wild grapevines, which at the time were in blossom. The country was of joyous appearance, and the lands contiguous to the river appeared of excellent friableness, and capable of producing every species of fruits. The river came down from some very high mountains through a spacious ravine which was penetrated by a bend from the east and northeast. At a gunshot aside from it, and outside the trees was discovered a pueblo or ranchería of the same Gentiles who were guiding our people. It was composed of various brush and bough shelters and of huts of a pyramidal shape covered with earth. On sighting their companions with the followers they were escorting, all came out to receive them: men, women, and children proffering their houses to the guests. The women came in modest garb, covered from waist to knee with close-woven and doubled nets. The Spaniards arrived at the ranchería, which must have consisted of thirty or forty families, and at one side of it a protective enclosure, made of branches and trunks of trees. Inside this, they gave us to understand, they took refuge to defend themselves from their enemies when they saw themselves attacked; a fortification inexpugnable to the arms in use among them.

These Indians are of good figure, well-built and agile. They go naked without more clothing than a girdle of *ixtle,* or very fine maguey fiber, woven in the form of a net. They take out this thread from a plant called *Lechugilla.* Their quivers, which they bind in between the girdle and the body, are of skins of wild cat, coyote, wolf or male deer, and their bows are two varas long. Besides these arms, they use a kind of war club of very hard wood, whose shape is like that of a short and curved cutlass, which they fling edgewise and it cleaves the air with much violence. They hurl it a greater distance than a stone. Without it they never go forth to the field, and if they see a rattlesnake or other noxious animal, they throw the *macana* at it and commonly sever it in half. According to the experience afterward in the continual discussions which our Spaniards had with them, they are of haughty temper, daring, covetous, great jesters, and braggarts, although of little valor; they make great boast of their powers, and hold the most respect for the most valiant. They greatly crave whatsoever rag, but when we have clothed different ones of them on repeated occasions, they would present themselves the following day stark naked.

There are in the land, deer, antelope, many hares, rabbits, squirrels, wild cats, and rats. The ring-necked turtle-doves abound, and so do the quail, calendar-lark, mockingbird, thrush, cardinal, and hummingbird, jackdaw, crow and hawk, pelican, gull, divers and other maritime birds of prey. There is no lack of ducks nor of geese, of different shapes and sizes. There is a variety of fish. The best are the flounder and the sole which besides being of delicate taste, are of extraordinary size and weigh from fifteen to twenty pounds. In the months of July and August one can catch as much bonito as one wishes. During all the year there are halibut, burga-os, horse-mackeral, dogfish, rays, mussels and cockles of all species. In the winter months the sardine runs in as great abundance as on the coasts of Galicia and Ayamonte. The principal sustenance of the Indians that inhabit the shore of this Port is fish. They eat much cockles, for the greater facility they have in catching them. They use balsas (rafts) of rushes, which they manage dexterously with a paddle or oar of two blades. Their harpoons are of some varas in length. The point is of bone, very much sharpened, inserted in the shaft of wood. They are so dexterous in hurling this that rarely do they miss their target.

Having reconnoitered the watering place, the Spaniards returned back on board the vessels. As these were found to be very far away from the estuary in which the river discharges, their Captains Don Vicente Vila and Don Juan Pérez resolved to approach it as closely as they could, in order to give less work to the men in the handling of the launches. These labors were too much hardship, for from one day to the next this aggravated and increased the fatigue of the few who remained on their feet.

Near the beach, on the side toward the east, a scanty enclosure was constructed, formed of a parapet of earth and brushwood. Two cannons were placed onto the parapet. They disembarked some sails and awnings from the packets, with which they made two tents, large enough for a hospital. At one side the two officers, the Missionary Fathers and the surgeon put their own tents. And everything being found in shape to receive the sick, they were brought from on shipboard in the launches and arranged in the tents as comfortably as possible.

But these caves were not enough to procure them health. They already lacked the medicines and diet, nearly all of which had been consumed during the sea voyage. The surgeon, Don Pedro Prat supplied in what manner was possible this lack with some herbs which he sought in the fields, with a thousand anxieties. Of the virtues of the herbs of which he had knowledge, and he himself was in as sore need of them as were the sick, since he found himself little less than prostrated with the same affliction as they. The cold made itself felt with rigor at night in the tents, and the sun likewise by day, alternations which made the sick suffer cruelly, two or three of them dying every day. This whole expedition which had been composed of more than ninety men was reduced to only eight soldiers and as many sailors able to attend to the protection of the boats, the working of the launches, guarding the camp, and caring for the sick.

There was no news of the expedition by land. The neighborhood of the Port had been searched, looking for tracks of a horseherd, but none were discovered and it was not known what to think of this delay. But on May 14, the Indians told some soldiers who were on the beach that from the direction of south of the Port some men were coming, armed as they: and explained very well by signs that they were coming mounted on horses. All were joyous at this news, which was verified from there in a short time, sighting the people and the packtrain of the first division of the expedition by land. They exchanged salutes with festive salvos from their weapons; later explaining with arms and voices their gladness, which was equal on both sides, since all hoped to find from the others relief in their needs. The men who had traveled overland had done so without having lost one man, and without bringing one sick one, after a march of two months, but on half rations, and with no more provisions than three sacks of flour, of which they were issuing as the entire daily ration two tortillas to each individual.

They rested that day close to the camp of the sick. They were furnished with food with which to regain their strength, and the officers agreed to move the camp close to the river which had not been done before because it had not seemed proper to divide the small force with which they found themselves employed at the guarding of the boats and of the men lodged on land. They also took into account the greater convenience and shortness of the transportation, so as not to fatigue excessively those who worked the launch, and because the lack of beasts of burden which compelled them to carry on their shoulders whatever was landed on the beach.

All were removed to the new camp, which was transferred one league further north, to the right of the river, on a hill of middle ground height. There they set themselves to attending the sick with greater care. The Surgeon, Don Pedro Prat, did not leave them an instant, and ministered with the utmost loving kindness. But seeing that he did not succeed in any betterment of them, and that it would come to a point where for lack of Mariners the two packetboats would find it impossible to put forth from the Port, there was serious thought of despatching one of the boats to San Blas with messages to inform the Most Excellent Sir Viceroy and the Most Illustrious Visitador-General of the state of both expeditions.

Don Juan Pérez, Captain of the *Príncipe (San Antonio)* was named for this purpose; Don Vicente Vila resolving to remain in San Diego until receipt of new orders and the reinforcement of men he needed to carry out that which his superiors might determine.

The packet discharged her cargo; part of the goods were transported to the camp, the rest were transshipped to the *San Carlos*. She was rigged out, and when ready to set sail, the Governor Don Gaspar de Portolá arrived with the second division of the expedition under his command on June 29.

He informed himself then of the state of affairs at San Diego, and, desirous that the expedition by sea should be carried out in its full effect, he proposed to give to Don Vicente Vila sixteen men from his command to pursue his voyage to Monterey. But as among them there was not one that was a sailor, Vila could not accept his offer. Particularly since he had lost all his ship's officers, boatswain, storekeeper, and coxswain of the launch and could not put his hand on anyone to replace them.

And the Governor, considering that the unexpected mishaps of the ships did not excuse him from pursuing his trip to Monterey by land, seeing that all of his troop and the rest of his retinue were well, and that he brought with his division 163 mules laden with provisions, counting also upon the assistance of food that the appointed packet *San Joseph* was to bring, which according to the arrangements and advice of the Most Illustrious Señor Visitador-General ought to be presumed to be already navigating toward the same destination, he decided to continue his march in search of that port without waiting for the season to get too far advanced, in order not to expose themselves to having the snows close the mountain passes which might be met on the way. Already it was known by the experience of that year that it snowed much, even at San Diego, whose mountains, those who had come by sea, saw snow-covered at their arrival in April of the same year.

In this understanding the Governor accelerated his arrangements, and proposed to the two army officers Don Pedro Fages and Don Miguel Costansó to follow in his company, with the soldiers who might find themselves in a state to do so properly—who at this time were six. The said officers accepted his offer. And after having sent off a report to the Most Excellent Señor Viceroy and to the most Illustrious Señor Visitador-General as to all that had so far befallen and was planned to be done, the packet *San Antonio* set sail with the letters on the ninth day of June, with only eight men for a crew.

In San Diego such an escort was left as seemed sufficient for the guard of the mission and of the sick, with the surgeon Don Pedro Prat, that he might continue to minister to them. There was also left an adequate number of horses and mules for the service of all. The Reverend Fathers Fray Junípero Sierra, Fray Juan Vizcaíno and Fray Fernando Parrón remained behind with the object of establishing that new *Doctrina* or Mission for the conversion of the Indians, although Serra obliged by the weariness and hardships he had endured to suspend his march, remained to await a vessel in which to travel to Monterey, which destination he had chosen. The Reverend Fathers Fray Juan Crespí and Fray Juan Gómez went with the expedition.

The expedition left San Diego on June 14, 1769.

The two divisions of the land expedition marched as one. The Commander so arranged matters this way in order for there to be enough of a horse herd and packs, since they carried only 100 packs of provisions and supplies, which he estimated to be necessary to ration all the men during six months, thus providing against a delay of the packets, although it was held to be impossible that in this interval some one of them should fail to arrive at Monterey.

On the marches the following order was observed: At the head went the Commandant with the officers, the six men of the Catalonian Volunteers who joined the expedition at San Diego, and some friendly Indians, with spades, mattocks, crowbars, axes, and other implements of pioneers, to chop open a passage whenever necessary. After them came the pack-train, divided into four groups with their muleteers, and an adequate number of presidial soldiers for their escort with each group. In the rear guard, with the rest of the troops and friendly Indians, came the Captain Don Fernando Rivera, convoying the horse-herd and the mule-herd for relays.

The soldiers of the presidio of Loreto in California, of whom justice and fairness obliges us to say that they worked infinitely on this expedition, use two sorts of arms, offensive and defensive. The defensive are the leather jacket and the shield. The first, whose make is like that of a coat without sleeves, is composed of six or seven thicknesses of white skins of deer, tanned, impenetrable to the arrows of the Indians since they are not discharged from a close range. The shield is of two thicknesses of raw bullhide. It is held with the left arm, and with it lances or arrows are deflected, the trooper defending himself and his horse. They use, beside the aforesaid, a kind of apron of leather, fastened to the pommel of the saddle and which lays over each side, which they call *armas* or protection, which cover their thighs and legs so as not to be hurt when running in the thickets. Their offensive weapons are the lance, which they manage dexterously on horseback; the broadsword, and a short flintlock musket which they carry thrust into and made fast in its sheath. They are men of much endurance and long-suffering under fatigue. They are obedient, resolute, agile, and we do not hesitate to say that they are the best troopers in the world, and including those soldiers who best earn the bread of the Majestic Monarch whom they serve.

It must be well understood that the marches of these troops with such an expedition, and with such obstacles through unknown lands and unused trails could not be long ones, leaving aside the other reasons which obliged them to halt and camp early, that is to say, the need of exploring the land one day for the next, so as to regulate the marches, according to the distance of the watering-places. And, to take into consideration the proper precautions, by setting forth again on special occasions in the evening, after having given water to the beasts in that same hour, with the positive information that in the following stretch there was no water or that the watering place was low, or the pasture scarce.

The rests were arrived at by the need of four in four days, more or less, according to the extraordinary fatigue brought on by the greater roughness of the road, the toil of the pioneers, or the straying of the beasts which were missing from the horse-herd; it being necessary to find them by their tracks. At other times, due to the necessity of attending the sick, when there were any, and with time there were many who gave up their strength to the continued fatigue, the excessive heat and cruel cold.

But the greatest risk of those travelers, and the enemy most to be dreaded, is this same horse-herd without which, indeed, the trip could not be made. In a country they do not know, these animals frighten themselves by night with incredible ease. To stampede them, in the language of this land, it is enough for them to discover a coyote or fox. A bird which flys by, the dust which the wind circulates—these are capable of terrifying them and making them run many leagues, precipitating themselves over *barrancas* and cliffs, without any human effort working to stop them.

Afterward, it cost immense toil to gather them again, and this was not always possible. Those that have not died by falling down precipices, or crippled themselves in their impetuous runaway remain of no service for a long time. But this expedition did not experience serious mishaps through this kind of casualty, thanks to the care and vigilance which were always observed, for although on some occasions the animals were stampeded, no fatality or damage followed, because the stampede was of short duration.

In the form and according to the method noted, the Spaniards executed their marches, traversing immense lands, more fertile and more pleasing the farther they penetrated to the north. All in general are peopled with a multitude of Indians, who came out to meet them and in some parts accompanied them one stage of the journey to the next; a people very docile and easily controlled, chiefly from San Diego onward.

The Indians in whom was recognized more vivacity and industry are those that inhabit the Islands and the Coast of the Santa Barbara Channel. They live in villages whose houses are of spherical form in the shape of a half orange, covered with rushes. They are up to twenty varas in diameter. Each house contains three or four families. The hearth is in the middle, and in the top of the house they leave a vent or chimney to give exit for the smoke. In nothing did these Gentiles contradict the affability and good treatment which were experienced in other times by the Spaniards who landed upon those coasts with the General Sebastian Vizcaino. They are of good figure and appearance, men and women; very much given to painting and staining the face and body. They use great headdresses of feathers, and some streamers which they bind up amid their hair, with various trinkets and beads of coral of various colors. The men go entirely naked, but in time of cold they wear some long capes of tanned otter skins and some mantles made of the same skins cut in long strips, which they twist in such a way that all the fur remains outside. Then they weave these strands one with another, forming a weft, and give it the pattern so mentioned.

The women go with more decency, bind around the waist tanned deer skins which cover them in front and behind more than halfway down the leg, and wear a small cloak of otter over the body. There are some with good features. These are the women who make the trays and receptacles of rushes, to which they give a thousand different forms and graceful patterns, according to the uses for which they are meant, whether it be for eating, drinking, storing their seeds, or other purposes. These peoples do not know the use of earthenware as those of San Diego use it.

The men work handsome trays of wood, with solid inlays of coral or of bone, and some vases of much capacity, narrowing at the mouth, which appear to be made with a lathe, and with this machine they could not come out better hollowed nor of more perfect form. They give the whole a luster which appears as the finished handiwork of a skilled artisan. The large vessels which hold water are of a very strong weave of rush, covered with pitch inside, and they give them the same form as our water jars.

In order to eat the seeds which they use in place of bread, they toast them first in great trays, putting among the seeds some pebbles or small stones heated until red. Then they move and shake the tray so it may not burn. Getting the seed sufficiently toasted they grind it in mortars of stone. Of these mortars some are of extraordinary size, as well-made as if they had the best steel tools. The constancy, attention to trifles, and labor which they employ in finishing these pieces are well-worthy of admiration. The mortars are so appreciated among themselves that when those dying leave behind such handiworks, they place them over the spot where they are buried, so that the memory of their skill and application may not be lost.

They inter their dead. They have their cemeteries within the same village. The funerals of their captains they arrange with great pomp, and set up over their bodies some extremely tall rods or poles, from which they hang a variety of utensils and possessions which were used by the dead. They likewise put in the same place some great planks of pine, with different paintings and figures, in which without doubt are explained the exploits and prowesses of the personage.

Plurality of wives is not lawful among these peoples. Only the captains have a right to marry two. In all their villages the attention was attracted to a species of men who lived like the women, kept company with them, dressed in the same clothes, adorned themselves with beads, pendants, necklaces and other womanish adornments, and enjoyed great consideration among the people. The lack of an interpreter did not permit us to find out what class of men they were, or to what ministry they were destined, though all suspect a defect in sex, or some abuse among those Indians.

In their houses the married couples have their separate beds on platforms elevated from the ground. Their mattresses are some simple bundles or mats of rushes, and their pillows are of the same bundles rolled up at the head of the bed. All these beds are hung about with similar mats, which serve for decency and protection from the cold.

The dexterity and skill of these Indians is surpassing in the construction of their canoes made of pine planking. They are from eight to ten varas in length, including their rake, and of a vara and a half beam. Into their construction enters no iron whatever, the use of which they know little. But they fasten the boards with firmness, one to another, working their drills just so far apart and at a distance of an inch from the edge, the holes in the upper boards corresponding with those in the lower, and through these holes they pass strong lashings of deer sinews. They pitch and caulk the seams, and paint the whole in sightly colors. They handle the boats with equal cleverness, and three or four men go out to the open sea to fish in them, as they have capacity to carry eight or ten men. They use long oars with two blades, and row with indescribable agility and speed. They know all the arts of fishing, and fish abound along their coasts, as has been said of San Diego. They have communication and commerce with the natives of the islands, whence they get the beads of coral which are currency in place of money through all these lands. Although they may hold in more esteem the glass beads which the Spaniards gave them, and offered in exchange for these whatever they had, like trays, otter skins, baskets, and wooden plates. More than anything they appreciate the clasp-knife or cutting instrument whose advantages over the tools of flint, they admire. It causes them much satisfaction to see use made of the axes and machetes, and the ease with which the soldiers, to make firewood, felled a tree with the said instruments.

They are likewise great hunters. To kill deer and antelope, they possess an admirable skill. They preserve the hide of the head and part of the neck of some one of these animals, skinned with care and leaving the horns attached to the same hide, which they stuff with grass or straw to keep its shape. They put this shell like a cap upon the head and go forth to the woods with this rare equipment. On sighting the deer or antelope, they drag themselves along the ground little-by-little, with the left hand. In the right they carry the bow and four arrows. They lower and raise the head, moving it to one side and the other, and making other movements so like these animals that they attract them without difficulty to the snare, and drawing them near, they discharge their arrows at them with certainty of hitting.

Among them were seen some pieces of broadsword, iron and fragments of wrought silver which, being of a small amount, seemed a novelty to our men. And asking them by signs how they acquired those things, they made signs and indicated they got them from the interior, toward the east. And, although New Mexico lies very distant in that direction, it is possible that these passed from hand-to-hand and that these trinkets may have come into their possession in time.

Their language is sonorous and of easy pronounciation. Some believe they find in it a certain connection with the Mexican (Aztecan) in that the L and T are frequently sounded as was observed among these natives. But those who know the Mexican can better infer as to this by the following words:

Words of the said tongue	Spanish
Nucchú	La cabeza
Kejuhé	el pecho
Huachajá	la mano
Chipuchú	el codo
tocholò	el sobaco
tononomò	el musio
pistocù	la rodilla
kippejuè	la pierna
acteme	el pie
tomol	lancha, ò canoa
apa	rancheria
temi	capitan, ò principal
amo	no

93

Numbers

pacà	uno
excò	dos
maseja	tres
scumu	quatro
itipaca	cinco
itixco	seis
itimasge	siete
malahua	ocho
upax	nueve
kerxco	diez

From the channel of Santa Barbara onward, the lands are not so populous nor the Indians so industrious, but they are equally affable and peaceable. The Spaniards pursued their trip without opposition up to the Sierra of Santa Lucia, which they worked to cross with much hardship. At the foot of said Sierra on the north side is to be found the Port of Monterey, according to ancient reports, between the Point of Pines and that of *Año Nuevo*. The Spaniards caught sight of said Points on October 1, 1769, and believing they had arrived at the end of their march the Commandant sent the scouts forward to reconnoiter the Point of Pines, in whose near vicinity lies said port in 36 degrees, 40 minutes north latitude. But the scant signs and vague signs which are given of it by the Pilot Cabrera Bueno—the only clue of this expedition, and the character of this port, which rather merits the name of bay, being spacious (in a likeness to Cadiz), not corresponding with the ideas which it is natural to form in reading the Log of the aforementioned Cabrera Bueno, nor with the latitude of 37 degrees in which he located it, the scouts were persuaded that the port must be farther north. They returned to the camp which our people occupied, with the report that what they sought was not to be seen in those parts.

The sick at that time numbered seventeen men crippled with scurvy. The season was advanced, the labors of guarding and night-herding the caballada, loading the pack-train, sentry duty in camp, and above all the reconnoissance and exploration of the regions, demanded, since they were naturally difficult, a greater number of people than there were in a condition to perform these services. So that the Commandant found himself doubtful as to the procedure it would be most fit to adopt, whether to wait at the spot for some vessel to appear, or to pursue the march in quest of the Port of Monterey. In this he considered the difficulties which have been mentioned, and not desiring to make the decision himself he called a council of his officers. They were unanimous with him in feeling that the march should be pursued. For if they did not arrive at the port and stopping place of the ships, to receive the food, utensils, and necessary munitions for the establishment which was to be made in Monterey, the aid which they so much needed could not be promised, nor would it be possible to form the establishment which had been ordered. And, last, that it was better to pass on in search of the port, which could not be far, according to all evidence, than to make a decision at once since there would always be in time to choose in case the sick should become worse or the number of them be increased.

It was resolved then to continue the expedition; on this occasion turning their backs on the port which was being searched for. The sick suffered much on this march. Some were recognized as in extremely bad shape. This retarded the march, as it was necessary to take a rest at each stage of the journey. At this time (the end of October) the rains began, and with them came an epidemic of diarrhea which spread to all without exception. It came to be feared that this sickness, which prostrated their strength and left the persons spiritless, would finish the expedition altogether. But it turned out quite to the contrary for as many as were afflicted and suffering with the scurvy; crippled, swollen in all their members and burdened with pains, began then to experience alleviation of their ills. Little by little the swellings went down, the pains ceased, they recovered the use of their members, and at last their perfect health, without any medicament.

The last day of October the land expedition came in sight of the Punta de los Reyes and the Farallones Islands of the Port of San Francisco, whose landmarks compared with those related by the Log of the Pilot Cabrera Bueno, and were found exact. Then it became evident that the Port of Monterey had been left behind, there being few who stuck to the contrary opinion. The Commandant, nevertheless, resolved to send men to reconnoiter the land as far as Punta de los Reyes. The scouts who were commissioned for this purpose found themselves obstructed by immense estuaries which run extraordinarily far back into the land, and were obliged to rack their brains to figure out how to make great detours. They used three days in this reconnoissance, and returned saying that according to the signs the Indians had given them they could not doubt that the Port of Monterey must be very near, and that surely some one of the packet boats had arrived at its destination, and they believed it to be the *San Joseph*. Little account was made of this information acquired by the medium of signs to take the place of speech. Nevertheless, not to leave with this doubt, it was resolved to go forward far enough to ascertain the fact. Having arrived at the end of the first estuary, and reconnoitered the land that would have to be followed to arrive at the Punta de los Reyes, interrupted by new estuaries, scant of pasturage and firewood, and having recognized, besides this, the uncertainty of the news and the misapprehension scouts had labored under, the Commandant with the advice of his officers, resolved to retreat to the Point of Pines, in hopes of finding the Port of Monterey and encountering in it the packet *San Joseph* or the *San Antonio* whose aid already was necessary since of the provisions which had been brought from San Diego little more remained than some few sacks of flour, of which a short ration was issued to each individual daily. With the powder and lead, the lack of other things was somewhat supplied, for hunting was plentiful, above all, that of geese and ducks, which in winter time abound extraordinarily in that land.

On November 11, there was put into execution the retreat in search of Monterey. The Spaniards reached said port and the Point of Pines on November 28. They maintained themselves in this place until the tenth day of December without any vessel having appeared in this time. For that reason and noting also a lack of food, and that there was snow falling on Sierra Santa Lucia, the Commandant Don Gaspar de Portolá obliged himself to decide to continue the retreat to San Diego, leaving until a better occasion the return to the undertaking.

On this retreat the Spaniards experienced some hardships and necessities, because they entirely lacked provisions, and because the long marches, which necessity caused them to make, to reach San Diego, gave no time to seek food by the hunt, nor did this game abound equally everywhere. At this point they killed twelve mules of the pack-train, on whose meat the men nourished themselves until they reached San Diego. On January 24, 1770 they arrived, all in health, at the new establishment.

They found their humble buildings in good condition enclosed with a palisade of trunks of trees, capable of a good defense in case of necessity. Many of the soldiers and sailors who stayed behind sick the preceding year had recovered from the fatal epidemic of scurvy, although the greater number of them, and these were the men who had first contracted the contagion on the sea, had hopelessly died.

The Reverend Missionary Padres were convalescing from the common sickness, as were also the Surgeon Don Pedro Prat, and Don Vicente Vila, for the contagion did not miss any person of those who were part of this expedition.

There were in San Diego, provisions of maize, flour, and seeds sufficient for the maintenance of those who composed the presidio for some months, but with the coming of sixty guests, it could not be counted upon to last for a very long time, and it was feared that if the ships should delay in bringing the provisions upon which they counted, those Spaniards might see themselves obliged by hunger to abandon entirely a conquest which, although very fortunate, had required so much toil, and so many lives. So as not to expose themselves to such discredit, the Commandant ordered that the Captain of the garrison of the Californias, with forty men, undertake a march to the (Lower California) peninsula, with the end of gathering up in its Missions the provisions that he could, and to bring the cattle on foot which, as was said at the beginning, had remained in Velicatá, and whose leanness had not permitted them to continue the march. This was shrewd foresight in that it looked to the actual number of consumers of the food which was on hand and to the means of enabling them to subsist thereafter, even though there should be failure of the provisions to come by sea, so important to carry into due effect the desired expedition to Monterey.

This detachment set forth, with the object stated on February 10, 1770. By this means an account was newly-given to the Most Excellent

Señor Viceroy and the Most Illustrious Señor Visitador-General, of the state of affairs, of what had happened, been seen, and discovered up to then by those Spaniards in their long trip in Northern California. Those who remained at San Diego awaiting the orders of said superiors found themselves reduced to a sad condition but they were consoled within a short time.

On March 23, the packetboat of His Majesty, the *San Antonio,* under command of its Captain and Pilot Don Juan Pérez, arrived and cast anchor in the Port of San Diego. It had set sail from San Blas, December 20, of the preceding year of 1769. It experienced during its voyage, severe storms and contrary winds which drove it to 400 leagues from the coast, and having found itself compelled to return in search of this coast to take on water, it made land at 35 degrees of north latitude. From there, turning its prow to the south and its left side to the coast, in search of some anchorage, it arrived at the Point Concepción in 34 degrees and a half of north latitude. This is the most westerly land of the Channel of Santa Barbara, and in its shelter they managed to take on water, close to a settlement of Indians, who gave them individual account of the expedition by land, saying by signs which were nowise vague how the strangers had passed going toward the north, and had passed returning, short of food, striking toward the south, mounted on their horses, which they acted out by putting themselves in like posture upon the barrels which the mariners put ashore, and making other demonstrations appropriate to indicate a man on horseback. They mentioned, likewise, the names of various soldiers, which, being recognized by some of the sailors, made it evident that these words were not sounded casually.

Captain Pérez, being convinced that the land expedition had retreated and in which he held no doubt, because he was not ignorant that the supplies could not have lasted them until then, determined to arrive at San Diego, to supply them with what they should need for the purpose of expediting his voyage to return to Monterey, his destination.

This was the measure which it was appropriate to take, and in fact the Commandant Don Gaspar de Portolá took it, nothwithstanding he found himself with few troops to undertake a second time, a march so extensive. But the knowledge which he had of the good disposition of the natives of those lands, and the hospitality which so exactly and in all places they had observed toward the Spaniards on their first entrada, took away this time all suspicion and gave them confidence. The march was decided upon, and taking the necessary provisions, was put into effect on April 17 of the current year, with only twenty men, between Leather Jacket Soldiers and Catalonian Volunteers, with their officer Don Pedro Fages.

In accordance with the orders given to him, the Engineer Don Miguel Costansó, embarked in the packet *San Antonio* on board of which also was transferred the Most Reverend Padre President, Fray Junípero Serra, and the vessel put to sea on April 16 of the same year.

All reached Monterey, those by land on May 23, and on May 31 of the same month the *San Antonio* cast its anchor in the same port and anchorage in which, 168 years before, was anchored the fleet of General Vizcaino, sent by the Count of Monterrey to explore these coasts, by order of our Lord Señor Philip Third. This port is found, as has been said, in 36 degrees and 40 minutes north latitude, at the descent of the Sierra of Santa Lucia, and on the north side. Its principal shelter is the Point of Pines, which stretches out (not from northeast to southwest, as the Pilot Cabrera Bueno located it, but) from northwest to southeast, and to the northeast shore of it is found the anchorage, in which whatever vessel can anchor in four, six, or eight fathoms. The bottom is of fine sand and good holding, since it is more or less close to land.

The Point of Pines which protects the anchorage from the northwest is all encircled with rocks and stone bluffs, but behind the rocks enters a beautiful beach bordered with sand dunes on its easterly bend, turning then to the northeast and north, up to a very great estuary with different arms, distant from the beginning of said beach more than three leagues. Then the coast follows turning to the northwest and west, of rather coarse earth adorned with groves, stony in places as far as Point Año Nuevo, which ends at 37 degrees and three minutes of north latitude. The anchorage remains surrounded by land on all sides except the northwest, where alone it lacks shelter.

The land which shuts in this immense bay, seen from the sea, forms an agreeable view. Looking to the south, can be seen the Sierra of Santa Lucia which lower and lower projects sundry hills, in ratio as they come down to the beach, their summits crowned with pines and covered with pasturage, presenting a magnificient amphitheater, made more colorful with the greenness of the different cañadas which break up the land and cause a wonderful variety and harmony to the eyes. This port has no running water, but sufficient water is found in a ravine or low place to the southeast of the landing, which is where the beach begins. In this place one passes a dry estuary which fills only at spring tides, and runs inland a considerable distance toward the east. This low place is very humid, and for this reason much grass grows in it, and is always green. So that, digging in whatsoever part, and opening wells, one will find fresh and good water, almost at the very surface of the earth. The water would be better if one cared to put into practice the same industry a little further inland in some little cañada of the many which come to flow there. For in them have been found various springs of excellent though scanty water.

On the northeast and east shore, the country stretches in beautiful plains which terminate at the Sierra. These have various small lagoons, though most of them are of brackish water. In some of them much salt crystallizes. The land generally is sandy, but there are many low places of excellent crumbly soil. To the south of the port, at a distance of two short leagues, is a spacious cañada, through which the river called Carmelo flows, where there are some fields of tall coarse grass which entirely hide a man on horseback, proof of the fierceness of the land. Its products are valuable, because there are walnuts, hazelnuts, and cherries as in Europe; black-berries, roses, and good grass every place.

In the Sierra are mostly stout oaks and live oaks, which produce good acorns, pines which bear cones, and piñons in abundance, forests of juniper, of cypress, and various other trees.

The natives of Monterey live in the Sierra. Those nearest the beach are distant from it about a league and a half. They come down at times and go forth to fish on little rafts of cattail rushes. But the fisheries cannot be their principal livelihood, and they resort to it only when the chase profits them little. Game abounds much in the interior of the Sierra, above all the antelope and deer. These Serranos (mountain Indians) are extremely docile and peaceful. They never used to come to visit the Spaniards without bringing them a good treat of game, which was generally composed of two or three deer or antelope, which they offered without demanding nor even asking anything in return. Their good disposition has given to the Reverend Missionary Padres well-founded hopes of winning them over to the Faith of Christ.

On these coasts, fish abound no less than in the Santa Barbara Channel and Port of San Diego. The cub whale and sea lion are numerous and with time the fishery for the former might perhaps be facilitated in that same bay.

In that land was built, according to the order, a presidio and mission under the Advocacy of San Carlos, all cooperating with equal care and solicitude: troops, mariners, and their respective officers, toward the humble beginnings of so important an establishment. Having concluded the preliminary work on it, which was finished more precisely for the Reverend Missionary Fathers and the troops of the Presidio, and having projected the remaining work which ought to be done, the cargo of the packet was warehoused. The decision was made by the Commandant Don Gaspar de Portolá to embark on the packet with the Engineer Don Miguel Costansó, leaving in command the Lieutenant of Infantry Don Pedro Fages, as he was advised in his instructions. To help the troops in their work, nine mariners remained in Monterey as a reinforcement.

The *San Antonio* put forth from that port July 9 of this year, and arrived happily at San Blas, the first of August. And when the other packet the *San Carlos* arrived at the same port, which returned from San Diego, both were made ready to undertake a new voyage in the coming month of November to convey separately, by the interior Gulf of California, and by the South Sea, thirty Apostolic Missionaries with abundant stores of provisions, clothing, utensils and sacred vestments, for the purpose of sustaining the new presidios of San Diego and Monterey, with their respective missions, and to build others in the fertile countries which the land expedition traversed from Velicatá as far as the Port of San Francisco, situated in 37 degrees, 45 minutes, north latitude.

In this way the desired establishments of San Diego and Monterey have had their happy beginnings. And so we ought to also promise ourselves, to carry out those new missions which are going to be founded and grow under the protection and patronage of the Most Excellent Señor Marqués de Croix, Viceroy Governor, and Captain-General of this far-reaching Empire, whose mild rule his subjects praise, and the peoples live for in gratitude. But this symbol desired for so many years, and promoted many times with great preparations and costs, will without doubt be very grateful to the Majestic Monarch who wears the Crown of Spain, whose noble heart and religious piety Heaven rewards with raising up in his glorious Reign, Illustrious and Great men in all stations, Ecclesiastical, Military, and Political, to vie equally in fulfilling the high positions which he entrusts to their eminent ability and talents, never better employed than in procuring the Propagation of the Gospel and the public welfare of his Loyal and Loving subjects.

Mexico, October 24, 1770.   Don Miguel Costansó

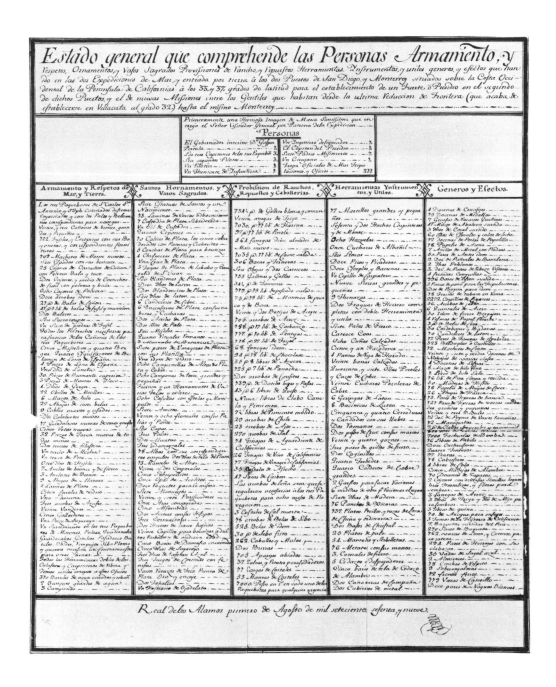

The Inventory or Summary of individuals, and all goods, arms, and supplies prepared on August 1, 1769, shipped or brought to Alta California by the two land expeditions and three sea arms of the force. The three vessels which left the Baja California Peninsula were the *San José, San Carlos,* and *San Antonio*. The *San José* sank, with all lives lost, somewhere off the coast of California. The document is reproduced by permission of the Huntington Library, San Marino, California. HM José de Gálvez, GA 532.

101

The Bibliography:

Any bibliography which would treat with the "Founding of Alta California" must necessarily be selective. There are literally several thousands of primary documents, or copies of documents within domestic and foreign archives. In instances those primary resources need mining by scholars. A few of the repositories rich in Spanish Colonial archival material are the Archivo General de la Nación and the Biblioteca Nacional, Mexico, D.F., the Museo Naval, and Archivo General de Indias in Spain; the U.S. Library of Congress, the University of Texas at Austin, the Bancroft Library at the University of California at Berkeley, the Henry E. Huntington Library at San Marino, California, and the Santa Barbara, California Mission archives.

Original or primary resources published, provide a wealth of information and reading on Spanish California, in the realm narrated by Miguel Costansó. The selection of items either for this general bibliography, or the items noted under the *Diarios,* is therefore, with the recognition that some important works might have been omitted, but with the intent of providing a well-rounded listing of primary source publications, and some outstanding secondary works.

Between March 6-9, 1969, the San Diego Congress of History, and the University of San Diego hosted an annual history convention which focused attention on this very subject: *The Founding of Alta California.* Papers delivered by the outstanding scholars of the Spanish Borderlands reflected the intensity of the work underway to provide new insight. Some of the papers delivered at that Convention are asterisked within the bibliography which follows. The San Diego Congress of History has plans to include these in a volume.

Bibliographies:

Barrett, Ellen C. *Baja Californa II, 1535-1964: A Bibliography of Historical, Geographical and Scientific Literature relating to the Peninsula of Baja California and to the Adjacent Islands in the Gulf of California and the Pacific Ocean.* Los Angeles: Westernlore Press, 1967. The first volume under the same title for the years 1535-1956, published by Bennett and Marshall, Los Angeles, 1957; a supplement for 1965-1966, by Katherine M. Silvera, and published by Baja Californianos of the Friends of Univ. of California at San Diego Library, La Jolla, 1968.

Bolton, Herbert Eugene. *Guide to Materials for the History of the United States in the Principal Archives of Mexico.* Washington: Carnegie Institution of Washington, Publication No. 163, 1913.

Castañeda, Carlos E. and Dabbs, J. A. (eds.). *Guide to the Latin America Manuscripts in the University of Texas Library.* Cambridge: Harvard University Press, 1939.

Chapman, Charles E., "The Literature of California History," *Southwestern Historical Quarterly,* vol. XXII, April 1919, pp. 318-332.

Chapman, Charles E. *Catalogue of Materials in the Archivo General de Indias for the History of the Pacific Coast and the American Southwest.* Berkeley: University of California, Publications in History, vol. VIII, 1919.

Geiger, Maynard J., O.F.M., *Calendar of Documents in the Santa Barbara Mission Archives.* Washington, D.C., Academy of American Franciscan History, 1947.

Guillen, Julio F. *Indice de los expedientes y papeles de la seccion de Indiferentes del Archivo Central de Marina.* Madrid: Instituto Historico de Marina, 1951.

Cowan, Robert Ernest and Cowan, Robert Granniss. *A Bibliography of the History of California, 1510-1930.* San Francisco: John Henry Nash, 1933. 3 vols. Vol. 4 by Robert Granniss Cowan, 1964.

Mecham, J. Lloyd (comp.), "The Northern Expansion of New Spain, 1522-1822: A Selective Descriptive Bibliographical List," *Hispanic American Historical Review,* vol. VII, 1927, pp. 233-276.

Robertson, James Alexander. *List of Documents in Spanish Archives Relating to the History of the United States, which have been printed or which are preserved in American Libraries.* Washington, D.C., Carnegie Institution of Washington, Publication No. 124, 1910.

Shepherd, William R. *Guide to Materials for the History of the United States in Spanish Archives.* Washington, D.C., Carnegie Institution of Washington, 1907.

Weber, Rev. Francis J. *A Select Guide to California Catholic History.* Los Angeles: Westernlore Press, 1966.

Biographical:

Bolton, Herbert Eugene. *Fray Juan Crespi: Missionary Explorer on the Pacific Coast, 1769-1774.* Berkeley: Univ. of California Press, 1927.

*Burrus, Ernest J., S.J. *Fernando de Rivera y Moncada: Explorer and Military Commander of both Californias.*

Claret, Pompeyo. *José de Gálvez, Marqués de la Sonora, Visitador-General de la Nueva España y fundador de California, Ministro de Indias con Carlos III.* Barcelona, 1963.

Drewes, Rudolph Herman, "Pedro Fages, California Pioneer," Master's Thesis, University of California, Berkeley, 1927.

Garcia, Luis Navarro. *Don José de Gálvez y la Comandancia General de las Provincias Internas del Norte de Nueva España.* Sevilla: Publicaciones de la Escuela de Estudios Hispano-Americanos de Sevilla, 1964.

Geiger, Maynard J., O.F.M., *The Life and Times of Fray Junipero Serra, O.F.M.,* Washington, D.C., Academy of American Franciscan History, 1959. 2 vols.

Geiger, Maynard J., O.F.M., "Biographical Data on the California Missionaries 1769-1848," *California Historical Society Quarterly,* vol. XLIV Dec. 1965, No. 4, pp. 291-310.

Geiger, Maynard J., O.F.M., (Transl. & annotator). *Palóu's Life of Fray Junipero Serra.* Washington, D.C., Academy of American Franciscan History, 1955.

Martinez, Pablo L. *Guia familiar de Baja California, 1700-1900; vital statistics of Lower California.* Mexico: Editorial Baja Calif., 1965.

Nuttall, Donald Andrew, "Pedro Fages and the Advance of the Northern Frontier, 1767-1782," Doctoral Dissertation, University of Southern California, 1964.

*Nuttall, Donald. *"Gaspar de Portolá: Disenchanted Conquistador of Spanish Upper California."*

Priestley, Herbert Ingraham. *José de Gálvez, Visitor-General of New Spain, 1765-1771.* Berkeley: University of California Publications in History, vol. 5, 1916.

*Servin, Manuel. *Miguel Costansó: Forgotten Founder of California.*

Shaffer, Ellen Kate, "Some Incidents in the Life of Captain Don Fernando (Javier) Rivera y Moncada," Master's Thesis, University of Southern California, 1954.

Tibesar, Antonine, O.F.M. (Transl.) *Writings of Junipero Serra.* Washington: Academy of American Franciscan History, 1955-1965. 4 vols.

Wilbur, Marguerite Eyre (ed.). *Juan Maria de Salvatierra by Miguel Venegas.* Cleveland: Arthur H. Clark Company, 1929.

*Wilson, Iris H. *"The Administrative Genius of José de Gálvez."*

Voyages of Discovery & Exploration:

Cabrera Bueno, Admiral José Gónzalez. *Navegación Especulativa y Práctica . . .* Impresa en Manila en el convento de nuestra Señora de los Angeles de la orden de Ñro Seraphico Padre San Francisco, año de 1734.

Carrasco y Guisasola, Francisco. *Documentos referentes al reconocimiento de las costas de las Californias, desde el Cabo de San Lucas al de Mendocino recopiladas en el archivo de Indias por D. Francisco Carrasco y Guisasola, coronel y capitan de fragata.* Madrid: Direccion de Hidrografia.

Chapman, Charles E., "Gali and Rodriguez Cermeño: Exploration of California," *Southwestern Historical Quarterly,* vol. XXIII, 1919-1920, pp. 204-213.

Gschaedler, André, "Mexico and the Pacific, 1540-1565, the Voyages of Villalobos and Legazpi and the Preparations made for them," Doctoral Dissertation, Columbia University, 1954.

Guillen, C. *Descubriemente por Tierra del Puerto de La Paz.* Madrid: Instituto Historico de Marina, 1943. (The logs, diaries, and documents related to the voyages of discovery).

Guzman-Rivas, Pablo, "Reciprocal Geographical Influences of the Trans-Pacific Galleon Trade," Doctoral Dissertation, University of Texas, 1960.

Holmes, Maurice G. *From New Spain by Sea to the Californias, 1539-1668.* Glendale: Arthur H. Clark Company, 1963.

Lorenzana, Francisco Antonio. *Historia de Nueva España, escrita por su esclarecido conquistador Hernan Cortes, aumentada con otros documentos, y notas, por el ilustrissimo Senor Don Francisco Antonio Lorenzana, arzobispo de Mexico, con las licencias necesarias.* Mexico: En la imprenta del superior gobierno. Ano de 1870. (the voyages of Cortes, and excellent reports of most expeditions to California up to the year 1769).

Mathes, W. Michael. *Vizcaino and Spanish Expansion in the Pacific Ocean.* San Francisco: California Historical Society, 1968.

*Mathes, Michael. *Sebastian Vizcaíno's Influence on San Diego.*

Mathes, W. Michael (ed.) *Californiana: Documentos para la Historia de la Demarcacion Comercial de California.* Madrid: Ediciones José Porrua Turanzas, 1965. 2 vols.

Moriarty, James R. and M. Keistman. *A New Translation of the Summary Log of the Cabrillo Voyage in 1542.* La Jolla: San Diego Science Foundation, Occasional Paper No. 2, 1963.

Portillo y Diez de Sollano, Alvaro de. *Descubrimientos y Exploraciones en las Costas de California.* Madrid: Publicaciones de la Escuela de Estudios Hispano-Americano de Sevilla, 1947.

Schurz, William Lytle, *The Manila Galleon.* New York: E. P. Dutton & Co., 1959.

Wagner, Henry Raup. *The Cartography of the Northwest Coast of America to the Year 1800.* Berkeley: University of California Press, 1937. 2 vols.

Mariners, Ships, and Ports:

Barnes, Esther, "The San Carlos, the Mayflower of the Pacific," Master's Thesis, University of California, Berkeley, 1935.

*Collins, William. *The Ships of the Move to Alta California.*

Cutter, Donald C. *Malaspina in California.* San Francisco: John Howell Books, 1960. (Excellent section on ships and shipbuilding).

Gardiner, C. Harvey, "The First Shipping Constructed in New Spain," *The Américas,* April 1954, vol. 10, no. 4, pp. 409-420.

Hittell, Theodore, "El Triunfo de la Cruz," *The Californian,* vol. 1, no. 1 Jan. 1880, republished by the California Historical Society as *El Triunfo de la Cruz, the First Ship built in the Californias,* Special Publn., No. 38, 1963.

Longstaff, F. V., "Spanish Naval Bases and Ports on the Pacific Coast of Mexico, 1513-1833," *British Columbia Historical Quarterly,* July-October 1952, pp. 181-189.

*Sayner, Donald, "Maping and Cartography of the Founding Period."

Taylor, Paul S., "Spanish Seamen in the New World During the Colonial Period," *Hispanic American Historical Review,* vol. V, 1922, pp. 631-661.

Tate, Vernon Dale, "The Founding of the Port of San Blas," Doctoral Dissertation, University of California, Berkeley, 1934.

Thurman, Michael E. *The Naval Department of San Blas: New Spain's Bastion for Alta California and Nootka, 1767-1798.* Glendale: Arthur H. Clark Co., 1967.

*Thurman, Michael. *San Blas: Bastion of the Pacific.*

The Geography & Environment of the Californias:

Baegart, Johann Jakob. *Observations in Lower California,* trans. by M. M. Brandenburg and Carl L. Baumann. Berkeley: Univ. of California Press, 1952. Other editions include those in German published in 1772 and 1773; the translation and arrangement by Charles Rau for the account in the Smithsonian Institution *Annual* Reports of 1863 and 1864, pp. 352-369; then separately published in Washington, D.C., in 1866.

Aschmann, Homer. *The Natural and Human History of Baja California from manuscripts by Jesuit Missionaries.* Los Angeles: Dawson's Book Shop, 1966.

Aschmann, Homer. *The Central Desert of Baja California: Demography and Ecology . . .* Berkeley: University of California Press, 1959.

Cook, Sherburne F., "The Extent and Significance of Disease Among the Indians of Baja California, 1697-1773," *Ibero-Americana,* vol. 12, No. 12, 1937, pp. 1-39.

Guzmán, Luis E., "A Geographical Study of the Llano and San Quintín Area," Master's Thesis, University of California at Los Angeles, 1950.

Hensen, Virgil Raymond, "Mission Valley, San Diego County, California: A Study in Land Use (Changing) from 1769-1960," Master's Thesis University of California at Los Angeles, 1960.

*Ives, Ronald, "Problems of Serra's Route from Loreto to San Diego."

Kroeber, Alfred Louis. *Handbook of the Indians of California.* Washington, D.C., Govt. Printing Office, 1925. Smithsonian Institution, Bureau of American Ethnology Bulletin 78.

Massey, William C., "Tribes and Languages of Baja California," *Southwestern Journal of Anthropology,* vol. 5, 1949, no. 3, pp. 272-307.

Massey, William Clifford, "Culture History in the Cape Region of Baja California," Doctoral Dissertation, Berkeley, 1955.

Spier, Leslie, "Southern Diegueño Customs," *American Archaeology and Ethnology,* vol. 20, 1923, pp. 297-358.

Sauer, Carl O. and Meigs, Peveril Meigs. *Site and Culture at San Fernando de Velicatá.* Publications in Geography, Lower California Studies, No. 1 vol. 2, no. 9, pp. 271-302, Sept. 30, 1927. Also in book Univ. Calif., 1927.

The Missionaries in Baja California:

Clavijero, Francisco Javier, S.J. *Storia della California* (1789) in *A History of Lower California,* transl., by Sara E. Lake and A. A. Gray. Stanford; 1937.

Bolton, Herbert Eugene, "The Black Robes of New Spain," *Catholic Historical Review,* vol. XXI, Oct. 1935, pp. 257-282; reprinted in *Wider Horizons of American History,* University of Notre Dame Press, 1967.

Burrus, Ernest J. (transl.) *Wenceslaus Linck's Diary of his 1766 Expedition to Northern Baja California.* Los Angeles: Dawson's Book Shop, 1966.

Chapman, Charles E., "The Jesuits in Baja California," *Catholic Historical Review,* vol. 6, April 1920, no. 1, pp. 46-58.

Downey, Mother Mary Margaret, "The Expulsion of the Jesuits from Baja California," Doctoral Dissertation, University of California, Berkeley 1940.

Ducrue, Benno. *Ducrue's Account of the Expulsion of the Jesuits from Lower California, 1767-1769,* edited by Ernest J. Burrus, S. J. St. Louis: Jesuit Historical Institute, 1967.

Dunne, Peter Masten. *Pioneer Black Robes on the West Coast.* Berkeley: Univ. of California Press, 1940.

Dunne, Peter Masten. *Black Robes in Lower California . . .* Berkeley: Univ. of California Press, 1952.

Dunne, Peter Masten, "The Expulsion of the Jesuits from New Spain, 1767," *Mid-America,* vol. 8, 1937, pp. 3-30.

Geiger, Maynard J., O.F.M., "Instructions Concerning the Occupation of California, 1769," *Southern California Historical Society Quarterly,* vol. XLVII, June 1965, pp. 209-218.

Hiltenbeitel, Paul H., "Franciscan Mission Colleges in Mexico," Master's Thesis, Xavier University, 1949.

*Kenneally, Rev. Finbar, O.F.M., "The Apostolic Colleges in Historical Perspective."

*McMorrow, Clyde H., M.D., "Mission San Fernando de Velicatá."

Meigs, Peveril. *The Dominican Mission Frontier of Lower California.* Berkeley: University of California Press, 1935.

Tichenor, Mother Helen Elizabeth, "The Opening of the Southern Missions of Baja California." Master's Thesis, University of California, Berkeley, 1923.

Weber, Francis J. *The Missions and Missionaries of Baja California: An Historical Perspective.* Los Angeles: Dawson's Book Shop, 1968.

The Threat to Alta California:

Bancroft, Hubert Howe. *History of Alaska, 1730-1885.* San Francisco: The History Company, 1886. Reprinted, New York, 1960. Excellent background on the Russian advance.

Bannon, Father John Francis. *Bolton and the Spanish Borderlands.* Norman: Univ. of Oklahoma Press, 1964. The best study of Bolton's approaches to the study of the borderlands; chapter on "Spanish Defensive Expansion."

Bolton, Herbert Eugene, "Defensive Spanish Expansion and the Significance of the Borderlands," in *The Trans-Mississippi West.* Boulder, Colorado: 1930, pp. 1-42, and reprinted in *Wider Horizons of American History,* University of Notre Dame Press, 1967, pp. 55-106.

Bolton, Herbert Eugene, "The Mission as a Frontier Institution in the Spanish-American Colonies," *American Historical Review,* vol. XXIII, Oct. 1917, pp. 42-61. Reprinted by Academic Reprints, Texas Western College, El Paso, 1960, and in *Wider Horizons of American History,* University of Notre Dame, 1967, pp. 107-148.

*Cutter, Donald, "Early Spanish Plans for the Occupation of Alta California."

Golder, Frank A. *Russian Expansion on the Pacific, 1641-1858.* Cleveland: Arthur H. Clark Co., 1914.

Gerhard, Peter. *Pirates on the West Coast of New Spain, 1575-1742.* Glendale: Arthur H. Clark Co., 1960.

*Nasatir, Abraham P., "International Rivalry and the Founding of Alta California."

Sanchez-Barba, Mario Hernandez. *La Ultima Expansion Espanola en America*. Madrid: Instituto de Estudios Politicos, 1957.

The First Years in Alta California:

Atherton, Lucien C., "The Early History of the San Diego Presidial District, 1542-1782," Master's Thesis, University of California, Berkeley, 1930.

Avilez, Alexander, "Population Increases in Alta California in the Spanish Period, 1769-1821," Master's Thesis, University of Southern California, 1955.

Bancroft, Hubert Howe. *History of California*. San Francisco: The History Company, 1884-1890. Vols. 18-24 in the *Works*.

Bolton, Herbert Eugene. *Historical Memoirs of New California by Fray Francisco Palou, O.F.M*. Berkeley: University of Calif. Press, 1926. 4 vols.

Davidson, George. *The Discovery of San Francisco. The Rediscovery of the Port of Monterey, the establishment of the Presido (sic) and the founding of the Mission of San Francisco*. From the Transactions and Proceedings of the Geographical Society of the Pacific, vol. 4, no. 2, May 1907.

Engelhardt, Zephyrin, O. F. M. *The Missions and Missionaries of California*. San Francisco: James H. Barry Company, 1913-1930. 5 vols and index (1916). In various editions. Rev. Engelhardt produced a number of volumes on the history of individual Alta California missions.

Priestley, Herbert I. (Transl.) *A Historical, Political, and Natural Description of California by Pedro Fages*. Berkeley: University of California Press, 1937; also in *Catholic Historical Review*, vol. IV, Jan. 1919, pp. 486-509; vol. V. April 1919, pp. 71-90.

Priestley, Herbert I. *Franciscan Explorations in California*, edited by Lillian Estelle Fisher, in the Spain in the New West Series. Glendale: Arthur H. Clark Co., 1946.

Stephens, Henry Morse and Bolton, Herbert Eugene (eds.) "The Founding of San Francisco," in *The Pacific Ocean in History*. Papers and Addresses presented at the Panama-Pacific Historical Congress at San Francisco, July 19-23, 1915. New York, 1917.

Townsend, Lawrence D., M.D., "Dietary Deficiency Diseases in the Period of Discovery," *San Diego Historical Society Quarterly*, vol. 10, Oct. 1964, no. 4, pp. 45-48.

Treutlein, Theodore E., "The Portolá Expedition of 1769-1770," *California Historical Society Quarterly*, vol. XLVII, Dec. 1968, no. 4, pp. 291-313.

Treutlein, Theodore E. *San Francisco Bay: Discovery and Colonization, 1769-1776*. San Francisco: California Historical Society, 1968.

Wagner, Henry Raup. *Early Franciscan Activities on the West Coast*. Los Angeles: *Historical Society* of Southern California, 1941, reprinted from article of same title in vol. 23, Sept.-Dec. 1941, nos. 3-4, of the *Quarterly*.

Watson, Douglas S. and Temple, Thomas Workman II (Transls.) *The Spanish Occupation of California . . . Junta or Council Held at San Blas . . .* San Francisco: Grabhorn Press, 1934.

Watson, Douglas (ed.) *The Expedition into California of the Venerable Padre Fray Junipero Serra and his Companions in the year 1769 as told by Fray Francisco Palóu*. San Francisco: Lawton Kennedy, 1934.

*Manuscript in possession of author.

The Diarios:
The sea expeditions from Lower California to San Diego in
Upper California:

The San Carlos (alias Toîson de Oro):

Captain Vicente Vila kept the log for the voyage from La Paz, which began on January 9, 1769, and ended at San Diego on April 29, 1769, although the log was maintained until May 12 of that year. Miguel Costansó, and Fray Fernando Parrón sailed with this voyage. Vila made frequent observations to the Cabrera Bueno *Navegacion Especulativa y Practica . . . ,* and to General Sebastían Vizcaíno's "notes."

See F. J. Teggart and Robert Seldon Rose, editors, "The Portolá Expedition of 1769-1770: Diary of Vicente Vila," *Publications* of the Academy of Pacific Coast History, vol. 2, no. 1, Berkeley, Univ. of Calif., 1911.

The *San Carlos* made a trip back to La Paz on August 24, 1770: if the log for that voyage exists it might well reflect the discussions of Costansó and Vila over the Vizcaíno, and Cabrera Bueno information they utilized to navigate to San Diego. See Del No. 353, letter from Costansó to De Gálvez in that collection at the Huntington Library.

The San Antonio (alias El Príncipe):

Captain Juan Pérez maintained a log for the voyage to Alta California. The ship left Cabo San Lucas on February 15, 1769 with Fray Francisco Gómez, and Fray Juan González Vizcaíno, on board. The vessel arrived at San Diego on April 11, 1769. She left that port on July 9, and arrived at San Blas on July 30, 1769. The *San Antonio* embarked with provisions and badly-needed supplies from San Blas in December 1769, and arrived at San Diego on March 23, 1770.

The diaries of Captain Pérez, at least for these early voyages, do not appear to have been located.

The diario maintained by Fray Juan González Vizcaíno, from February 6 to April 6, 1769, was edited by Arthur Woodward, as *The Sea Diary of Fr. Juan Vizcaîno to Alta California in 1769,* Los Angeles, Glen Dawson, 1959.

The San José (alias El Descubridor):

This vessel, built at San Blas, and commissioned in July 1768, with 180 tons burthen, had been scheduled as a part of the supply line to Alta California. She left Cabo San Lucas in May 1770 captained by Domingo Antonio Callegari and the second-pilot Don Felipe Jimenez, and most likely sank off the coast of California rather than off Cabo San Lucas as some historians suggest.

Some records such as ship manifests were prepared at Loreto, between May and August 1769, and are in the José de Gálvez collection at the Huntington Library, San Marino, California. Other documents related to the *San José* are situated in the collections of the Institute of Latin American Studies, the University of Texas at Austin, and the Archivo General de Indias, particularly the Audiencia de Guadalajara sección. The significance of this vessel has been somewhat underestimated, and would make a most relevant study.

The land expeditions from Lower California to San Diego in
Upper California:

The first expedition led by Captain Fernando Javier Rivera y Moncada left the Mission of San Fernando de Velicatá on March 24, 1769, and arrived at San Diego May 14, 1769.

The commander, Captain Rivera probably kept a diary, although this author has not found any record of such.

As for the numerous diaries kept by Fray Juan Crespí, sources include Alan K. Brown, "The various Journals of Juan Crespí," *The Américas,* vol. XXI, April 1965, pp. 375-398; Rev. Maynard J. Geiger, "The Arrival of the Franciscans in the Californias, 1768-1769—according to the version of Fray Juan Crespí, O.F.M., *The Américas,* vol. 8, Oct. 1951, pp. 209-218; and Charles J. G. Piette, "Two Unknown Manuscripts Belonging to Early California," *The Américas,* vol. III, July 1946, pp. 91-101; Oct. 1946, pp. 234-243; January 1947, pp. 368-381.

In his article "Diarios of Early California, 1769-1784," *The Américas,* vol. II, no. 4, April 1946, pp. 409-422, Fr. Piette indicates seven journals kept by Fray Crespí. His first "Diary of the first expedition by land for the exploration of the Port of San Diego," appears in *Fray Francisco Palóu's Historical Memoirs of New California . . . ,* edited by Herbert Eugene Bolton, University of California Press, 1926, in volume 2, pp. 42-104.

The second expedition led by Governor Gaspar de Portolá and Padre Junípero Serra left Velicatá on March 9, 1769, and arrived in San Diego on July 1, 1969.

Donald Eugene Smith and Frederick J. Teggart, editors, "Diary of Gaspar de Portolá during the California Expedition of 1769-1770," *Publications* of the Academy of Pacific Coast History, vol. 1, no. 3, 1910, University of California at Berkeley. The Governor's diario covers the journey from Santa María in Lower California on May 11, 1769 to the arrival in San Diego on July 1; then the trip from San Diego which began on July 14 in search of the port of Monterey which ended in San Diego on January 24, 1770.

The diario of José Cañizares titled "Diario de Joseph de Cañizares, Villacata to San Diego, July 3, 1769," in the California transcripts, Bancroft Library, University of California at Berkeley was translated and edited by Virginia E. Thickens and Margaret Mollins, and appeared as "Putting a Lid on California: An Unpublished Diary of the Portolá Expedition by José de Cañizares," *California Historical Society Quarterly,* vol. 31, June 1952, no. 2, pp. 109-123; no. 3, Sept. 1952, pp. 261-270; and no. 4, Dec. 1952, pp. 343-354. Cañizares opened his journal on March 24, 1769 and closed it on May 14, of that year.

The diary of Fray Junípero Serra, began at the Mission of Loreto in Lower California and has been published on several occasions. Charles Fletcher Lummis made an incomplete translation and printing in *Out West,* vol. XVI, March 1902, pp. 293-296; April 1902, pp. 399-406; May 1902, pp. 513-518; June 1902, pp. 635-642; July 1902, pp. 69-76, which he recorded as the expedition of Portolá from Loreto to San Diego, March 28 to June 30, 1769. Another somewhat incomplete account appeared as his diario edited by the Franciscan Missionaries of Mary, published in Providence, Rhode Island in 1936. More recently Benjamin Franklin Dixon translated and edited the Diario, the *Journal of Padre Serra from Loreto . . . to San Diego . . . : (as) a new grass roots translation.* Published by Don Diego's Libreria, San Diego, 1964 and 1967.

The Expedition in search of the Port of Monterey, and those journeys which followed shortly thereafter:

Miguel Costansó kept a remarkable diary of the expedition led by Governor Portolá from San Diego to search for the Port of Monterey. He gave it the title of "Diary of the Journey made by land, made to the north of California by order of His Excellency the Marqués de Croix, Viceroy, Governor and Captain-General of New Spain, Etc., Etc.,; by instruction of the Most Illustrious Don Joseph de Gálvez, of the Council and Court of His Majesty in the Supreme Council of the Indies, Inspector-General of all the Tribunals, Royal Exchequers, and Departments of Finance of his Majesty in the Same Kingdon, and Intendent of the King's Army, Etc., Etc.; performed by the troops detailed for this purpose under the command of the Governor of the Peninsula of Califor-

Puerto de La Paz sobre la Costa Oriental de California . . . de la Latitud de 24° 20 minutos, Miguel Costansó, 1768.

Plano del Puerto y Nueva Poblacion de San Blas sobre la costa de la Mar del Sur situado en 28° y 30' de Latitude Septentrional y 266° de Longitude contados desde el Meridiano de la Ysla del Fierro y Levantado por el Teniente de Yngenieros Don Miguel Costansó en 23 de Mayo de 1768. Los Numeros de la Boca del Puerto e interior de el expresan brazas de Fondo la Varriacion del Yman en esta Costa de 5° Noroeste.

HOGARTH PRESS is grateful to
many fine people who were of
great help in all phases of the
birth of this book.
JOHN BRUCKMAN was its father;
DR. RAY BRANDES delivered it;
ROBERT O. DOUGAN and the staff of
Henry E. Huntington Library were in attendance
as were
ZELLERBACH PAPER COMPANY: Larry Hardy
TYPOGRAPHY: Photo Typo/Graphics
ART DIRECTOR: Hal Shulem
BINDING: Bela Blau

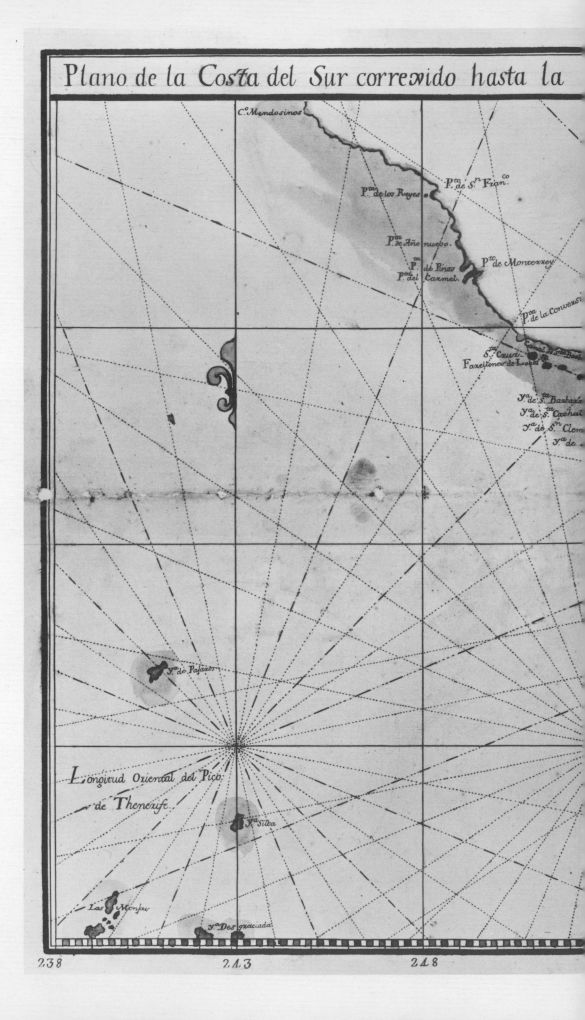

C.º Mendosinos

P.ᵗᵃˢ de los Reyes

P.ᵗᵒ de S.ⁿ Fran.ᶜᵒ

P.ᵗᵃ de Año nuebo.

P.ᵗᵃ de Pinos

P.ᵗᵒ de Monterrey

P.ᵗᵃ del Carmel.

P.ᵗᵃ de la Conversi.ᵗ

Canal de S.ᵗᵃ Barb.ᵃ

S.ᵗᵃ Cruz

Farellones de Lobos

Y.ᵃ de S.ᵗᵃ Barbara

Y.ᵃ de S.ᵗᵃ Corthal

Y.ᵃ de S.ⁿ Clem

Y.ᵃ de

Y.ᵃ de Pajaros

Longitud Oriental del Pico
de Thenerife.

Y.ᵃ Silva

Las Monjas

Y.ᵃ Desgraciada

238   243   248